Debating Climate Change

Science in Society Series

Series Editor: Steve Rayner
Institute for Science, Innovation and Society, University of Oxford

Editorial Board: Gary Kass, Anne Kerr, Melissa Leach, Angela Liberatore, Stan Metcalfe, Paul Nightingale, Timothy O'Riordan, Nick Pidgeon, Ortwin Renn, Dan Sarewitz, Andrew Webster, James Wilsdon, Steve Yearley

Business Planning for Turbulent Times
New Methods for Applying Scenarios
Edited by Rafael Ramírez, John W. Selsky and Kees van der Heijden

Debating Climate Change
Pathways through Argument to Agreement
Elizabeth L. Malone

Democratizing Technology
Risk, Responsibility and the Regulation of Chemicals
Anne Chapman

Genomics and Society
Legal, Ethical and Social Dimensions
Edited by George Gaskell and Martin W. Bauer

Marginalized Reproduction
Ethnicity, Infertility and Reproductive Technologies
Lorraine Culley, Nicky Hudson and Floor van Rooij

Nanotechnology
Risk, Ethics and Law
Edited by Geoffrey Hunt and Michael Mehta

Resolving Messy Policy Problems
Handling Conflict in Environmental, Transport, Health and Ageing Policy
Steven Ney

Unnatural Selection
The Challenges of Engineering Tomorrow's People
Edited by Peter Healey and Steve Rayner

Vaccine Anxieties
Global Science, Child Health and Society
Melissa Leach and James Fairhead

A Web of Prevention
Biological Weapons, Life Sciences and the Governance of Research
Edited by Brian Rappert and Caitrìona McLeish

Debating Climate Change

Pathways through Argument to Agreement

Elizabeth L. Malone

publishing for a sustainable future

London • Sterling, VA

First published by Earthscan in the UK and USA in 2009

ISBN   978-1-84407-828-8 hardback
         978-1-84407-829-5 paperback

Typeset by MapSet Ltd, Gateshead, UK
Cover design by Susanne Harris

For a full list of publications please contact:

Earthscan
Dunstan House
14a St Cross Street
London EC1N 8XA, UK
Tel:+44 (0)20 7841 1930
Fax: +44 (0)20 7242 1474
Email: earthinfo@earthscan.co.uk
Web: **www.earthscan.co.uk**

22883 Quicksilver Drive, Sterling, VA 20166-2012, USA

Earthscan publishes in association with the International Institute
for Environment and Development

A catalogue record for this book is available from the British Library

Library of Congress Cataloging-in-Publication Data

Malone, Elizabeth L., 1947-
Debating climate change : pathways through argument to agreement / Elizabeth L.
Malone.
    p. cm.
 Includes bibliographical references and index.
 ISBN 978-1-84407-828-8 (hardback) — ISBN 978-1-84407-829-5 (pbk.) 1.
Climatic changes—Social aspects. 2. Climatic changes—Political aspects. 3.
Climatic changes—Government policy—International cooperation. I. Title.
 QC903.M35 2009
 363.738'74—dc22

                                                              2009007565

At Earthscan we strive to minimize our environmental impacts and carbon footprint
through reducing waste, recycling and offsetting our CO_2 emissions, including those
created through publication of this book. For more details of our environmental
policy, see www.earthscan.co.uk.

This book was printed in the UK by TJ International,
an ISO 14001 accredited company. The paper used
is FSC certified and the inks are vegetable based.

To Richard Brown, kind and wise mentor;
and to Frank, Andrew, Ellen and Tyler,
for their non-stop love and support

Contents

Electronic supplementary material for this book is available online at www.earthscan.co.uk/dcc in the form of a PDF file containing a first-stage analysis for each of the 100 arguments considered in the text.

List of Figures and Tables

Figures

Tables

Climate Change in the Spotlight

The arguments that are crowding thick and fast onto stages in academia, think tanks, policy circles, climate negotiations, mass media and the blogosphere exhibit passionate advocacy – and also, unfortunately, a great deal of passionate invective against other arguments. Environmentalists who want to have energy produced only from renewable sources paint those who would continue fossil fuel use and expand nuclear power as deep-dyed villains or, at best, addicts to damaging substances. In turn, environmentalists may be derided as 'true believers' who have their heads buried in the sand and simply do not understand how the system works. Among those who judge that technological solutions are urgently needed, animosity smoulders or flares up between those who say that implementation of existing technologies will be sufficient to achieve drastic emissions reductions and those who assert that entirely new technologies will be essential in this 'battle' against climate change.

Each camp accuses others of not understanding either the science or the scope of the problem and faults the others for advocating actions that will not address or fix the problems. Propositions, treaties, multilateral activities, experimental markets, technologies, voluntary actions – all have been termed either essential solutions or wrongheaded, inappropriate, inadequate, based on incorrect or pernicious frameworks, failures, futile, and worse.

Both the sense of urgency and the number of proposed actions about global climate change are escalating, even as the global economy is nose-diving. There are hot debates about whether carbon markets should be mainly cap-and-trade systems, incentives or mandates of renewable energy; whether offsets of any kind should be permitted; how to include carbon sinks in plants and soils; how much energy-related behaviours can be expected to change; how much we can tinker with the present energy system to make it more efficient; the role of nuclear power – and, oh yes, whether climate change is even something to be worried about.

What strikes me over and over again is that, despite what we might call a sea change in attitudes about climate change, especially in the US, the basic arguments have not changed since the early years of the debate. Not at all.

They stem from the same worldviews – indeed, how could they not? – and reflect the same types of tactics.

This book uses evidence largely taken from the first decade after countries agreed to the United Nations Framework Convention on Climate Change – 1992 to 2003. But the arguments contained in these documents are the same arguments current today.

As a sound-bite-sized preview of the book, here are the arguments that people made in 1992 to 2003, characterized in the text to follow as 'argument families':

1   Climate isn't changing; the science is incorrect or incomplete.
2   Climate is changing, but people needn't do anything. Either human beings are not to blame and/or they will find ways to adapt as it happens, just as they have in the past.
3   Climate change is a subject of scientific investigation, and further research will provide knowledge.
4   The world needs more of the tools of modernity to address climate change, particularly development and implementation of effective treaties, conventions, protocols and other policy mechanisms.
5   The world needs more of the tools of modernity to address climate change, particularly new technologies for the energy system.
6   The world needs more of the tools of modernity to address climate change, particularly reduction of emissions, from all sources.
7   The world needs more of the tools of modernity to address climate change, particularly preparation for adaptations that will be necessary.
8   The world needs more of the tools of modernity to address climate change, particularly creation of markets for environmental goods.
9   The world needs more of the tools of modernity to address climate change, particularly all feasible mitigation and adaptation actions.
10 Climate change is another instance of rich and powerful countries preserving their hegemonic positions.
11 Climate change reflects human beings' broken relationship with the natural world.

Looking at the current controversies, we can see the same arguments. Arguments about cap-and-trade schemes make the #4 argument that large-scale policy actions (preferably international) will accomplish the needed emissions reductions. If governments set a limit on total emissions (the cap) and allocate permits to emit only up to the cap, companies that produce lower levels of emissions can sell their emissions permits to others, thus creating a carbon market and ensuring that cheap reductions will be undertaken first. (If it were cheaper to reduce emissions than to buy a permit, the company would make the reductions.) Advocates for such a system cite the successful US cap-and-trade system that addressed acid rain; the Environmental Defense Fund, for example, says, 'The policy stopped acid rain. See how it can stop global warming.' Opponents cite recent experience with the initial failures of the European Union's cap-and-trade system as well as general opportunities to profit by the system without contributing to its goals. Opponents may advocate a carbon tax instead of a cap-and-trade system and so make the same argument about the primacy of large-scale policy actions. The disagreement is about tactics. Although these debaters oppose each other, often passionately, they actually agree more than they disagree.

A second example is the global conversation about new technologies, especially energy technologies. This is obviously a #5 argument, with a further fleshing out of details about investments in basic research and development, government and industry roles in implementing new technologies, what the new technologies should or could be, and whether or not the technologies we already have can meet emissions-reduction needs. Again, there are fierce arguments that are just about technologies: about the feasibility and desirability of individual classes of technologies (for example nuclear and biofuels) and about whether we need to substitute technologies in the current system or completely transform the way we produce energy. However, these debaters agree that climate change is happening, that it must be addressed, and that technology is all or most of the answer.

Economists, too, find matters to quarrel about – even those who agree that climate change is a worrisome issue that must be addressed. A December 2008 discussion in the UK, called 'The hot debate', staked out four positions:

1   That 1–3 per cent of GDP should be spent on this urgent problem, because the benefits of avoided change are very large.
2   That only a modest amount should be spent on mitigation, bearing in mind that the uncertainties about climate change could mean that our fears are groundless, and that, moreover, the benefits are uncertain.
3   That action is urgent and well founded, because much can be done fairly cheaply; innovation will also have knock-on benefits; we have a short window of opportunity to go down the right path; acting now prevents harm to systems with great inertia; and risks on the side of action are knowable.
4   That we need decisive action but should start with research and development (for new technologies), a carbon tax, and an effort to persuade China to commit to mitigation. (*Financial Times*, 2008)

Again, these economists exhibit much agreement here, although they disagree about timing, the policy instrument (taxes or cap-and-trade or both) and particular actions. (Interestingly, the moderator closes by saying they 'disagree so violently'.) They are all making #4 and #5 arguments, and all have the standard economic worldview of costs and benefits. Their disputes are – or should be – amenable to dialogue, negotiation and compromise rather than being bedrock, line-in-the-sand differences.

Or let's look at what might seem to be an entirely new argument: that climate change will affect national security, either as a 'force multiplier' or as a driver of migration, resource conflicts (such as wars over water) and food/water scarcity. Any of these can cause unrest and conflict, including physical violence. An additional impact that is worrisome involves the degradation of infrastructure (for example, military coastal facilities, offshore drilling operations and electricity grids). Issues that are tied to national security discussions are energy security and food security. These arguments and proposals for action are mostly in the modernization argument families (#4–9); studies done by and with participation of military or intelligence professionals, not surprisingly, typically recommend actions within the political sphere (#4) and in developing new technologies (#5), though also in conducting research and analysis (#3). Here, for instance, are the recommendations from a 2007 study by the US CNA Corporation, involving a Military Advisory Board of retired generals and admirals:

1   The national security consequences of climate change should be fully integrated into national security and national defence strategies.
2   The US should commit to a stronger national and international role to help stabilize climate changes at levels that will avoid significant disruption to global security and stability.
3   The US should commit to global partnerships that help less developed nations build the capacity and resilience to better manage climate impacts.
4   The Department of Defense (DoD) should enhance its operational capability by accelerating the adoption of improved business processes and innovative technologies that result in improved US combat power through energy efficiency.
5   The DoD should conduct an assessment of the impact on US military installations worldwide of rising sea levels, extreme weather events and other possible climate change impacts over the next 30 to 40 years.

The first three recommendations reflect the political argument, the fourth the technological argument and the last the need for further research to determine what the impacts are projected to be.

One last topic of lively discussion and (dis)agreement is the role of rapidly developing countries, particularly China and India. Such countries do not have emissions-reduction responsibilities under the Framework Convention on Climate Change but have become important emitters – indeed, China is now the largest emitter of greenhouse gases. The US cited the lack of such countries' participation in emissions-reduction goals as a reason not to ratify the 1997 Kyoto Protocol. But China and India, arguing from a cumulative-emissions perspective (in other words, that the developed countries have emitted more than 80 per cent of the carbon in the atmosphere today), refuse to establish targets for reducing greenhouse gas emissions. This is the same argument that has been maintained since the 1980s – argument family #10.

What of those who have made arguments based on the need to repair or re-conceptualize human beings' relationship with Nature (#11)? Environmentalists who have passionately tried to 'speak for Nature' and advocated draconian measures to dismantle extractive technologies and practices are still in evidence. Theirs are still mainstream voices in climate change debates. However, many are now arguing *within* the modernization (arguments 4–9) worldview. They argue against the use of nuclear power to reduce greenhouse gas emissions (because of radiation damage issues), favour the exclusive use of renewable energy (as 'natural'), and caution that the implementation of carbon dioxide capture and storage technologies will simply maintain our 'addiction' to fossil fuels.

The continuity of the arguments encourages me to think that this book will help to sort out the differences in arguments made about climate change and point to ways to move the debate forward so that actions can be agreed. There are links among people, their interests and their beliefs almost everywhere. Emphasizing these links, these things in common, can provide the basis for programmes, policies and activities that large majorities can support.

References

CNA Corporation (2007) *National Security and the Threat of Climate Change*, CNA Corporation, Alexandria, VA, http://securityandclimate.cna.org/

Financial Times (2008) 'The hot debate', *The Financial Times*, 1 December, www.ft.com/cms/s/0/97f7df34-b9c3-11dd-99dc-0000779fd18c.html?nclick_check=1

1

Trying to Make Sense of Disparate Arguments about Climate Change

A confession: I am a social scientist. I came to social science because of climate change. This may seem odd – a social scientist interested in a physical science problem – so let me explain. From a background in English language and literature, I focused on technical writing and editing (teaching and doing) for 20-plus years. Eventually, I found myself co-editing a fascinating assessment of social science relevant to climate change, then writing about the social-institutional issues raised in the assessment. Although I think that climate change is happening and that people are causing much of the change, those are not the questions that I found really intriguing. No, what got my attention and interest were two questions: how do we, as societies, decide that scientific knowledge is valid? And can we as a world of human societies ever hope to agree on what to do about a global issue in which many kinds of knowledge may be contested?

How do we as societies decide that scientific knowledge is valid?

For some – scientists and non-scientists – the process seems clear. Scientists do research and make discoveries about how the world works. These discoveries then become the basis for other discoveries – for example, the discovery of the virus that causes an illness becomes the basis for a vaccine. At some point, scientific discoveries may become the basis for policy. For example, the discovery of damage to workers from contact with a toxic material becomes the basis for regulations limiting use of that material or requiring protective clothing.

But what social scientists like Sheila Jasanoff and Brian Wynne (1998) have found is that the real process doesn't conform to this neat version of it. And perhaps this shouldn't be surprising. Politicians and manufacturers are not necessarily waiting for the next scientific articles (or even the reports of research they actually sponsored) to tell them what to do. And the converse is true, too: scientists are not necessarily waiting for politicians or manufacturers to tell them what they should research.

Jasanoff and Wynne, who study the social processes by which scientists work and scientific results become common knowledge, point out that, instead of a kind of knowledge hand-off, the process of knowledge creation and communication involves social processes at every step. Even as scientists perform research, they examine results as members of a scientific community and formulate hypothetical explanations. Peer review and participation in scientific meetings are highly socialized ways in which scientific results and their implications change and evolve. In fact, science thrives in the give-and-take of conferences and published debates. Scientists are professional sceptics, insisting on being able to duplicate experiments and examine data before accepting new findings and theories.

Into this complex social system comes the second question.

Can we as a world of human societies ever hope to agree on what to do about a global issue in which many kinds of knowledge may be contested?

How can we as a world of human societies ever hope to agree about what – if anything – to do about a global issue? This question also involves the first question, since if we argue about whether the issue itself has some basis in knowledge, we are likely to disagree about what actions to take. But this broader question brings in all kinds of social patterns, institutional behaviours and communication pathways that affect our ability both to talk in fruitful ways about an issue and to agree on actions.

Not the facts, but the debate

So this book revolves around what are, I believe, more interesting questions than whether climate change is actually happening. Moreover, I am not primarily concerned about analysing greenhouse gas emissions as such, whether from industrial processes or building insulation or exhausts – or even about urban planning or land uses or conservation of natural resources. My focus is on how we talk to each other about each of these issues and many other issues bound up in climate change. I have confessed already that I am a social scientist. Now I confess further that I came to the climate change issue not because climate change itself is compelling (although it is), but because of its characteristics as a problem: it's one of the biggest problems around, involving all of the most complex social science issues: How do we come to define issues and problems? How do we deal with them? How does social change come about?

Talking, that almost ubiquitous human practice, holds the key to many of the answers to these questions. Who are the people in the climate change debate and what are they talking about? Most people have by now heard the terms 'global warming' and 'climate change', but understanding the issue implies much more than just hearing the terms. The complicated scientific explanations that are often given as 'answers' to people's bewilderment do little or nothing to increase that understanding, much less make the issue relevant. And those who try to make the issue relevant give wildly conflicting messages.

There are the 'doom and gloom' messages. For example, we hear that there will be devastating hurricanes. Drought will become widespread. Ice sheets will melt and land – including whole islands – will be submerged in rising seas. Animal and plant species will move or die out. New diseases will proliferate.

There are the 'why should I worry?' messages. For example, we hear that warmer temperatures will open up new agricultural lands. People will spend less to heat their houses. Everybody likes warmer weather. And, whatever happens, people have proven that they can adapt to changes in climate. Furthermore, any change that might occur is probably attributable to natural – not human – causes.

A host of other messages circulate in the debate as well. This book will discuss and categorize the arguments made in order to identify areas of agreement and disagreement.

Even the so-called scientific evidence regarding climate change comes in many forms. Consider the following four disparate statements (sources are listed at the end of this chapter):

1   *Changes in the atmospheric abundance of greenhouse gases and aerosols, in solar radiation, and in land surface properties alter the energy balance of the climate system. These changes are expressed in terms of radiative forcing, which is used to compare how a range of human and natural factors drive warming or cooling influences on global climate. Since the Third Assessment Report (TAR), new observations and related modelling of greenhouse gases, solar activity, land surface properties and some aspects of aerosols have led to improvements in the quantitative estimates of radiative forcing.* (IPCC, 2007, p2)

2   *The core of the climate change problem is as simple as it is daunting: we now know that it will be impossible for the whole world to obtain – or even to approach – the emissions levels of the industrialized countries without gravely endangering our planetary life-support systems. In the US, emissions average over five tons of carbon per person per year; even in more efficient European economies, average emissions exceed two tons of carbon yearly. Yet global annual emissions must fall by more than 50 per cent – to a third of a ton per person or less – if atmospheric greenhouse gas (GHG) levels are to be stabilized in this century. ... Thus, if the developing nations follow the energy-technology pattern of the rich countries, the planet faces the risk of catastrophic climate change.* (Baer, 2002)

3   *All this is not to say we shouldn't act. We must act, and in every way possible, and immediately. We must substitute, conserve, plant trees, perhaps even swallow our concerns over safety and build some nuclear plants. We stand at the end of an era – the hundred years' binge on oil, gas and coal, which has given us both the comforts and the predicament of the moment. George Woodwell, a Woods Hole marine biologist, who is currently studying the world's forests to discover just how fast they are dying, says we are committed to a warming of several degrees. But if we do not dramatically cut carbon dioxide and other greenhouse gases, the atmosphere will never reach a steady state and 'there is virtually no action that can be taken to assure the continuity of natural communities'. Even the countries that think they wouldn't mind warming of a degree or two for a longer growing season can't endure an endless heating. There is, Woodwell says, 'no question that we've reached the end of the age of fossil fuels'. The choice of doing nothing – of continuing to burn ever more oil and coal – is not a choice, in other words. It will lead us, if not straight to hell, then straight to a place with a similar temperature.* (McKibben, 1999, p146)

4   *Ambiguous scientific statements about climate are hyped by those with a vested interest in alarm, thus raising the political stakes for policymakers who provide funds for more science research to feed more alarm to increase the political stakes. After all, who puts money into science – whether for AIDS or space or climate – where there is nothing really alarming? … But there is a more sinister side to this feeding frenzy. Scientists who dissent from the alarmism have seen their grant funds disappear, their work derided, and themselves libelled as industry stooges, scientific hacks or worse. Consequently, lies about climate change gain credence even when they fly in the face of the science that supposedly is their basis.* (Lindzen, 2006)

The first quotation is from the most recent 'Summary for policymakers' in a book-length report of the scientific Intergovernmental Panel on Climate Change (IPCC) – careful, technical language accompanied by a highly stylized diagram of the climate and influences on it. The second is from a scientist who studies energy resources and use to examine the equity issues in possible emissions limitation schemes. The language is more understandable than that in the IPCC text; the evidence is a comparison of per-person emissions. The third is from a book called *The End of Nature* by a social scientist who quotes a natural scientist, using apocalyptic language. The fourth is from an article in the *Wall Street Journal*, with a scientist-sceptic questioning the 'alarmism' of the climate science community, accompanied by an illustration of a globe with sun-like rays coming out of it.

These writers, all scientists, use different arguments, evidence and language to talk about the implications of climate change. Specialized language (a reader who wanders into the text of the first example may well wonder what radiative forcing actually is) contrasts sharply with poetic description, third person with first person viewpoints, and quantitative charts with pure text.

Other voices in the debate are even more varied, bringing in diverse topics such as the overall economy, consumption and inequality. Some, perhaps environmental advocates or industry organizations, accuse various opponents of politicking (politicians and interest groups), practicing 'junk science' (researchers) and despoiling the Earth (all of us). Many feel that, if the public doesn't understand the science of climate change, it won't be motivated to take action. However, despite continuing efforts to educate the public, surveys show strong evidence that the public remains fairly uninformed about this fairly complex topic. Others think that the whole abstruse body of knowledge is a house of cards, a hoax or a scheme to get more research funding.

Here is a sampling of questions from a web chat featuring Kevin Trenberth, an atmospheric scientist from the National Center for Atmospheric Research (*Washington Post*, 2007):

1   *I live in Northern Virginia, where a prediction of two inches of snow causes school closures, government delays and almost universal panic. For days up to last night, the best that meteorology can buy predicted that it would start snowing at 4.00am in the area. Well, as of 8.00am, there is no snow (just some sleet) and a bunch of kids happy not going to school. My point is, if a simple forecast for the next few hours is missed, why should we believe in climate forecasts that will happen decades from now?*

2   *While I appreciate the value of double- and triple-checking in science, really, this consensus on anthropogenic global warming has been largely in place for between five and 10 years. But oil industry lobbyists and sociopathic conservatives ensured the public would be confused enough to doubt the science for a decade (Exxon alone spent $8 million doing this). What can our country learn from this ignominious period of our history about the value of listening to science when it comes to, well, scientific issues?*

3   *I am still sceptical about what man can do to stop global warming. We had two full ice ages before one plant/car was built. Every time you breathe, go to the bathroom or clap the planet heats us [sic]. Plus, the rate the planet is heating up isn't abnormal or out of line with history. Short of leaving the*

*planet and shutting down our economy, I don't see any steps
we can take that will make any difference.*

4   *Even if global warming is not caused by man, why wouldn't
we want to take steps to save our finite resources and live on a
cleaner planet? Green technology exists and, if eased into use,
will not cripple our economy. The US is the biggest polluter, by
far, on the planet. Other countries have emission standards in
place right now that far exceed our own, and their economies
are doing great (see Japan, their fuel emission standards and
the efficient cars they drive in order to meet those standards).
It's time for the US consumer to demand better; time for
lawmakers to help make it happen.*

One person doubts scientific capabilities to predict weather and climate
accurately; the next is ready to grant scientists authority in just this area. The
third feels that people won't make a difference unless they give up everything,
perhaps including the planet. The fourth says, sure, we can make a difference
and we have plenty of reasons to take action with or without climate change.

These disparate voices are just a sampling, and they are all voices from the
US. But we can look more broadly still, at a globalized world, where people
have a myriad of pressing concerns that may have nothing to do with climate
change or may be bound very tightly with the issue. Many societies and
countries are struggling with armed conflicts, poverty, disease and the vagaries
of world markets. Far from focusing on reducing greenhouse gas emissions,
they may instead race to build coal-fired plants to produce energy so they can
produce goods for the marketplace, both at home and abroad. They may see
calls to protect the environment as just one more way that rich nations want to
hold back poorer nations. Here are three of these voices:

1   *The adverse effects of climate change, climate variability, sea-
level rise, and associated phenomena such as the increase in
the intensity and frequency of hurricanes and other extreme
weather events continue to threaten the sustainable development, livelihoods and very existence of SIDS [small island
developing states]. For example in 2004, over 3000 persons
were killed in Haiti as a result of Tropical Storm Jeanne. That
same year Hurricane Ivan destroyed or damaged over 90 per
cent of the houses in Grenada and caused over US$815
million in damages or twice the GDP of that country. For
SIDS the adverse impacts of climate change are real, immediate and devastating. The failure of countries to reduce
domestic greenhouse gas emissions means that the vulnerability of SIDS will continue to increase and that adaptation to
climate change must continue to be a major priority for them.
We call on States that have not done so to ratify and fully*

implement the Kyoto Protocol, and for all States to take further urgent action to reduce domestic greenhouse gas emissions, including through the development and increased use of renewable energy. (Hunte, 2006)

2 *A very simple approach would be for nations to agree on an ad hoc per capita entitlement to which all countries will agree to converge. This entitlement could be anything like 0.5tC, 1.0tC or 1.5tC. The higher the entitlement, the better it would be for both developing countries and industrialized countries, because then developing countries could go up to higher per capita emissions while industrialized nations would not have to go down to levels that looked impossible to them. ... In any case, the purpose of entitlements is not to force every nation to come down to the same level of per capita carbon dioxide emissions, which industrialized countries like the US will probably find impossible to reach as long as they remain locked into a fossil fuel energy economy, but to create an equitable framework in which all nations can work together with the assurance that each person is entitled to equity in economic activities and there is sufficient scope for cooperation between the rich and poor countries so that both can move towards a carbon-free energy economy.* (CSE Factsheet, 1998)

3 *China is a developing country with a relatively low level of economic development and insufficient capability in technology development. Thus China is simultaneously facing the pressures of both economic development and environmental protection. As one of the non-Annex I Parties to the Convention, and in order to honour effectively the commitments stipulated by the Convention, China needs developed country Parties to provide assistance to it in terms of funds, technologies and capacity building in line with their obligations under the Convention, so as to strengthen China's capacity for the mitigation of and adaptation to climate change and improve the level of relevant studies.* (Government of the People's Republic of China, 2004)

In the first of these, a representative of the Association of Small Island States (AOSIS) points out the extreme vulnerability of small islands to the climate impacts of sea-level rise and severe storms. In the second, a public interest organization in India proposes an approach based on a concept of equal rights to the global environment. In the third, the Chinese Government reminds the Parties to the United Nations Framework Convention on Climate Change that China is not obligated to reduce its emissions without help from the more industrialized and wealthier countries.

In all of these excerpts and in many other written and spoken texts, represented in this book and elsewhere, people are trying to make sense of what they hear and read. They try to attach and fill in with knowledge they already have; they find confirmation of opinions they already hold; they connect with issues they already care about. They interpret new information in the context of their daily activities, livelihoods, possessions and relationships.

But if everyone understands climate change issues in idiosyncratic ways, where can we find or how can we develop a general sense of whether or not climate change is real, whether people are the culprits, how bad the impacts of climate change might be, and what (if anything) we could or should do? Coming out of the trees – indeed, out of the thick underbrush – and attempting to gain a forest-level perspective seems to be an impossible task.

And how to start? In arguments, we normally try to sort out the evidence, see where it leads and make a decision. This is a fairly straightforward and successful way of resolving issues when everyone in the argument agrees about the boundaries of the argument – what the issue is – as well as what the goals of any action may be and what the context of the whole debate is.

The impulse to find the 'right' or 'true' facts and inferences is strong. We like our problems and solutions simple. These preferences are clearly articulated in the kinds of questions put to scientists, seeking definitive answers about the nature and extent of climate change, its impacts, and the methods and costs of addressing it. In our private lives, appeals that seem based on clear and overriding principles may trump others with more complex rationales.

Unfortunately, it's often hard to draw clear lines. Even our everyday lives are full of situations where 'the truth' is debatable. And even with all the facts in hand, the best path forward is often not self-evident.

Climate change is an issue that defies simple analysis or accounting. Thousands of reports are crammed with data and information, but nothing we can say about the future is demonstrably true beyond the shadow of a doubt. And even if we take the scientific consensus as truth (or the closest to truth we will get), what to do to mitigate or adapt to climate change is still an issue on which people hold an extremely wide range of strongly felt opinions.

If we have as our goal achieving the 'right' or 'true' viewpoint that everyone should come to, we are doomed to disappointment. The arguments made are so diverse in their assumptions and focus that sorting them all out to arrive at the truth will be as fruitless as trying to figure out who started the name-calling among a group of children.

The very complexities of the climate change issue, however, along with the urgency that is becoming a prominent feature of the debate, are prompting us to do more than just trust an amorphous sorting-out process. If climate change presents serious risks, we ought to be up and doing something now.

Despite the difficulties, then, we should not give up on the debate. Instead, we can do what we do whenever 'the truth' is an unrealizable goal but the issue is important: we can try to come to agreement on courses of action (or inaction) that are at least acceptable to most debaters. This is the process that enables democracies, many industrial organizations and other groups to move forward, to find their way through contentious issues.

One thing we can do is to study the processes by which people debate and come to agreement. This is, by its very nature, a social process.

Elements of Arguments

I propose in this book to examine the wide range of arguments on climate change together, accepting that each has some validity and that all have something to say to each other. Instead of trying to get out of the trees and look at the whole forest, we can stay in the forest but examine the trees so as to see how they relate to one another, what commonalities and patterns can be seen, and what we can learn about the whole forest from an 'inside' perspective.

As a starting point in our quest for sense-making, let us begin with a relatively simple issue in order to begin to analyse a multi-participant debate. Let us take the issue of where to go on a family vacation.

The Smiths, parents and children, start a conversation in which everyone knows that the spring break is coming up (in other words they have a set time in March or April), they don't have the money to do anything but drive a reasonably short distance, one family member doesn't want a beach trip, and another has to have access to the internet wherever he goes. In such circumstances, each family member can propose a destination, argue for it on the basis of cost, time to destination and back, and the fun (or even educational value) of various activities while there. Although the debate may be lively, each family member knows that he or she has a stake in actually going on the vacation and is working towards the goal of getting to agreement on a destination that will be acceptable to everyone else while being especially fun for him or her.

The Joneses, on the other hand, faced with the same decision and discussion, find that the family members may not share the same goals or accept the same constraints. Perhaps one member sees the spring break as an opportunity for a family vacation, another sees it as an opportunity to catch up on work around the house, yet another wants to be with friends ('hanging out') all week, and the fourth member wants to find a way to reconcile all these views. The family needs time together, says one. I need my personal space, says another. Spring break is just another week, says the third. Why can't we all get along? says the fourth. Here the family has trouble agreeing on the basic terms of reference and the goal, much less any criteria for meeting that goal. They find they are always at square one.

These two families represent different stages and ways of entering into a debate. The Smith family may be a hierarchy (for example, the parents set the expectations and the children are too young to have their own agendas or know that resistance is futile) or just perhaps an assembly of very harmonious people. The second family, the Joneses, may have teenagers who are starting to flex independent muscles within the family, divergent viewpoints about what a vacation could do to or for family harmony (based on a parent's negative memories or the family's collective experience of conflicts while on vacation), or the 'too-busy syndrome' spotlighted in media reports, or perhaps is just an assembly of inharmonious people (which happens even in families).

The point of this simplified illustration is that several elements of a debate matter very much in its prospects for resolution – and especially for swift resolution. Elements include, certainly, the varying authorities of the participants in the debate, the degree to which the content of the debate matters to each participant, acceptance of the evidence (logic, facts and so on) that a debater uses to make points, the worldviews of the various participants, and the acceptability of the proposals themselves. Let's consider each briefly, as they are the heart of the more extended discussion in this book.

The varying authorities of the debaters

In a debate, whether it's a family discussion or an international negotiation, how much authority is claimed by or granted to a speaker (or writer, as the case may be) is important for how much weight will be given to her or his argument. Parents in a family normally have much more authority than the children, as they are older, more experienced and control most of the resources. But of course in some families children have considerable authority – granted to them by parents or accruing because of circumstances (for example, inheritance directly to them or special talents that are fostered). In country-level negotiations, economic or military power often bolsters authority, as do sets of alliances. These differences can often be seen in the people who show up to a negotiation; delegations with more people, knowledge and resources have obvious advantages in the negotiations. However, in these kinds of debates, as well as in many others, one or more participants may possess or accrue authority because of knowledge they have (from experience, scientific research or spying, for example) or because they are arguing from moral principles that other parties acknowledge as valid (even when the other parties do not acknowledge the validity of other elements of the argument).

The degree to which the content matters to participants

Even when one debater has almost all the authority in the group, he or she may not care about the outcome of the debate sufficiently to make a strong argument; he or she may simply cede (or may care about one point – for instance just the fact of going on vacation – but not about others – for instance where to go). Another who has little authority may argue so passionately as to convince others that his or her proposal should be adopted, despite any misgivings. A debater who cares may make appeals that are beside the point to bolster an argument (for example 'you owe me this') or persist in arguing beyond the stamina of the other participants. Of course, it is also quite possible that these tactics will simply backfire, and those with higher authority will both veto the proposal and develop an aversion to future proposals from the same person. Parallel phenomena happen at the level of international negotiations.

Acceptance of the evidence

Each debater must offer reasons why the claims and proposals he or she makes should be accepted by the others in the debate. These may consist of facts ('Did you know that X destination costs $50 less per night, on average, than Y?'), of logic, of appeals to known preferences, of attempts to point out the moral or ethical dimensions, and so on. What happened last time may be invoked as evidence of what may happen this time. Or assertions of organizational or personal characteristics (for example, the hotel staff are great or Uncle Bill never wants to do anything fun when we go to see him) may bolster a claim or proposal. In an international negotiation, each delegation shows up with a carefully designed strategy, complete with a more-or-less logical argument and more-or-less elaborate evidence to back up that position. Later chapters in this book will have more to say about how evidence may or may not support a claim or proposal as well as how such connections are used in the climate change debate. For now, we note that only very seldom would one debater's statement be accepted without some kind of evidence to back it up. In fact, arguing about the evidence may derail or stand in for arguing about the issue itself.

Worldview

Each participant in a debate comes to it with some assumptions about how the world works and how societies function (and should function). For some, the world is a place run by a benevolent God who takes care of the Earth and its people. People are stewards of the Earth and caretakers of each other. For other people, the world is a place where people are in competition with each other for the resources of the Earth and for power and wealth generally. Choices of friends and enemies are strategic decisions, based on who can help or hinder each individual. In terms of families (on vacation or not), one worldview may assume a hierarchy, with a father as decision-maker, a mother as homemaker, and children as obedient and well behaved. Another worldview is that the family members, whoever they are, nurture each other in a more egalitarian fashion. George Lakoff (2002) uses these two views of a family to explain the differences between Republicans and Democrats in the US – and, not incidentally, why the two parties often talk past one another instead of engaging in dialogue.

The acceptability of a proposal

Explicitly or implicitly, every debate includes proposed actions (or no action). Even when other elements of a debate may be hotly contested, participants may be able to offer proposals for action that can be agreed to by most or all other debaters. If one of our families engaged in a formal debate, one member might argue for 'Resolved: the Jones family should schedule several local family outings during the spring break.' Such a proposal might be compelling to family members with different interests who yet want to demonstrate at least some commitment to family solidarity. An international negotiation must usually offer something to all parties; if not, stalemate may be the result (or an unsatisfactory settlement that festers until the issue erupts again). Thus, the arguments for a particular proposal may be based on intrinsic qualities of the proposal (it's the right thing to do, logic or facts lead to this course of action, and so forth) or on extrinsic factors (this is the only action that can be agreed on, it offers something to all parties, and so forth).

When we return to a more extended and climate-change-focused discussion of these factors, we will trace them back to the ancient Greek philosopher Aristotle, who presumed that the goal of every debate was to arrive at the truth and that each element contributed to moving towards that goal. The ideal argument would satisfy other debaters in all of these elements and thus express the truth. Conversely, there may be debates in which participants agree on nothing and thus no truth can be arrived at.

The possibilities for debate about a new type of problem can be arrayed along a spectrum. At one end of a spectrum of possible responses, the participants throw up their hands and refuse to deal with the situation. They deny, rationalize or despair. At the other end of the spectrum, they immediately take action born out of total agreement about what to do. Between these theoretical 'nothing' and 'everything' responses, individuals, groups and societies debate definitions, the existence of a problem, the extent of the problem and the potential strategies for dealing with it.

Let's return to our example of vacations. Family debates are not simple to analyse, but they have several advantages as first-order sites to look at the ways people debate and come to agreement. First, families typically share some elements of their lives: a dwelling (sometimes more than one), some activities – such as eating, game-playing and inside jokes – and resources. Second, they know each other. Theoretically, each member knows about the habits, preferences, moods and triggers of the others. (Children famously know how to make their parents happy enough to grant their requests – and also how to needle them, to make them angry.) Third, families often share a worldview, perhaps including political leanings, religious beliefs, a view of science, feelings about the natural world and so on.

These commonalities and mutual knowledge can clear some of the contextual undergrowth out of the way so that the content of the debate can form more of the analytic focus. When conducting research, scientists look for factors that are the same so they can study one factor or a small number of factors that vary. The smaller the number of factors that vary, the more confident the researcher can be that the results of the study are valid. Studying a family, a more-or-less homogenous group, may allow a scientist to design the research so that the results can be stated with high confidence.[1]

For other debates, agreement about any of the elements discussed above cannot be taken for granted. In the climate change debate, people who are involved come from all walks of life and widely divergent cultures. They may share almost nothing: political view, religion, economic class, knowledge or behaviours. They have different views about how the world works and about how the world and societies *should* work. When they engage in dialogue and debate, they may find that they seem to be totally opposed, with nothing in common except a willingness to debate. They may find that they have to engage in endless side debates about the meanings of terms, the roles to be played by various countries or people, the functions of the natural world in human terms, and how equity bears on the debate. They may become so frustrated or angry that they withdraw from the debate. For many who are interested in the issue, the complexity of the issues and the cacophony of the debate may make it hard for them even to join the discussion.

So the kind of sorting out that we will do in this book will identify the various strands and elements in the debate and the patterns that the arguments form. As the patterns become visible and connected to other patterns and issues – for example, the issues collected under the term globalization – we can start to make sense of both the climate change issue and the debates that cluster around it.

I hope I have made clear by now that I am not focusing on the questions of whether the climate is changing and whether or not people are causing climate change. These questions are just two of many that are being debated under the umbrella of climate change. Other questions deal with how people should use the Earth's resources; whether technologies contribute most to our wellbeing or to environmental degradation that harms us; whether economic growth is always good; what our responsibilities are to our countries, other countries, and our descendents; and how much it would cost to lessen or eliminate our releases of greenhouse gases.

This sort of 'melting pot' debate is more than the sum of its individual parts, and we need to look at both the whole debate and its parts in order to find our way through it.

Motivation for the Book

Why should we bother? Well, in a world being knit closer and closer together – notably by fast transportation and information technologies – we all have a larger and larger stake in solving problems and resolving issues. When foreign markets experience a downturn, ours does too. When a new disease appears, we are all at risk. When power plants spew sulphur dioxide, places downwind (maybe even across oceans) get acid rain. If the climate changes, everyone will be affected.

So we should all be interested in figuring out how to argue better and more productively – and how we can discern points of agreement that might help us to build more agreement. This is not an easy process. Families, clubs, agencies, governments – groups and organizations of all kinds – often find themselves bogged down or stymied in negotiations, sometimes by issues that seem totally beside the point. But the difficulty of coming to agreement is more than matched by the importance of doing so. The alternatives are, in the main, negative: war and other conflicts, shortages of goods where they are needed, and environmental destruction.

In the climate change issue, we do have a starting point: the agreement of most countries of the world embodied in the United Nations Framework Convention on Climate Change (UNFCCC), agreed to in 1992. Its basic tenets are worth repeating here:

> *Article 2: The ultimate objective of this Convention and any related legal instruments that the Conference of the Parties may adopt is to achieve, in accordance with the relevant provisions of the Convention, stabilization of greenhouse gas concentrations in the atmosphere at a level that would prevent dangerous anthropogenic interference with the climate system. Such a level should be achieved within a time-frame sufficient to allow ecosystems to adapt naturally to climate change, to ensure that food production is not threatened and to enable economic development to proceed in a sustainable manner.*
>
> *Article 3: In their actions to achieve the objective of the Convention and to implement its provisions, the Parties shall be guided,* inter alia, *by the following:*
>
> 1 *The Parties should protect the climate system for the benefit of present and future generations of humankind, on the basis of equity and in accordance with their common but differentiated responsibilities and respective capabilities. Accordingly, the developed country Parties should take the lead in combating climate change and the adverse effects thereof.*
> 2 *The specific needs and special circumstances of developing country Parties, especially those that are particularly vulnerable to the adverse effects of climate change, and of those Parties, especially developing country Parties, that would have to bear a disproportionate or abnormal burden under the Convention, should be given full consideration.*
> 3 *The Parties should take precautionary measures to anticipate, prevent or minimize the causes of climate change and mitigate its adverse effects. Where there are threats of serious or irreversible damage, lack of full scientific certainty should not be used as a reason for postponing such measures, taking into account that policies and measures to deal with climate change should be cost-effective so as to ensure global benefits at the lowest possible cost. To achieve this, such policies and measures should take into account different socioeconomic contexts, be comprehensive, cover all relevant sources, sinks and reservoirs of greenhouse gases and adaptation, and comprise all economic sectors. Efforts to address climate*

change may be carried out cooperatively by interested Parties.

4   *The Parties have a right to, and should, promote sustainable development. Policies and measures to protect the climate system against human-induced change should be appropriate for the specific conditions of each Party and should be integrated with national development programmes, taking into account that economic development is essential for adopting measures to address climate change.*

5   *The Parties should cooperate to promote a supportive and open international economic system that would lead to sustainable economic growth and development in all Parties, particularly developing country Parties, thus enabling them better to address the problems of climate change. Measures taken to combat climate change, including unilateral ones, should not constitute a means of arbitrary or unjustifiable discrimination or a disguised restriction on international trade.*

You might say that ever since the world's countries agreed to these principles, they've been arguing about what they mean and how they can be practically implemented. Moreover, although the central governments of most countries have signed on, not everyone within these countries agrees with the Convention, so the debate is larger than just 'how to do it'. The Conference of the Parties to the UNFCCC (comprising all the countries that signed on) has met 15 times, many reports have been issued and several agreements have been forged, notably the Kyoto Protocol. But their accomplishments may seem meagre to those eager to get on with reducing greenhouse gas emissions and setting up incentives and enforcement structures – or too much too soon for those who are sceptical of the reality or implications of climate change.

The remaining chapters in this book are about different ways to analyse arguments in the climate change debate. Using the categories sketched out above, I will be examining the features of actual arguments where agreement or disagreement can be seen. Then a social network analysis will 'map' the points of agreement in the arguments and point to pathways where further agreement may be forged.

Note

1   Of course, research that takes one family (or a small number of families) as its unit of analysis may investigate factors at a more detailed level, and such a study has its own complexities, sometimes to the level of genetic material or cellular activities.

References

Sources for quotations (in order of citation)

IPCC (2007) 'Summary for policymakers', in S. Solomon, D. Qin and M. Manning (eds) *Climate Change 2007: The Physical Basis*, Cambridge University Press, Cambridge, UK

Baer, P. (2002) 'Equity, greenhouse gas emissions, and global common resources', in S. H. Schneider, A. Rosencranz and J. O. Niles (eds) *Climate Change Policy: A Survey*, Island Press, Washington, DC

McKibben, B. (1999) *The End of Nature*, Anchor Books, New York

Lindzen, R. (2006) 'Climate of fear', *Wall Street Journal*, 12 April, www.opinionjournal.com/extra/?id=110008220

Washington Post (2007) 'Science: Global warming and the government', *The Washington Post*, 13 February, www.washingtonpost.com/wp-dyn/content/discussion/2007/02/12/DI2007021200686.html

Hunte, J. (2006) 'Statement by Dr the Hon. Julian R. Hunte, SLC, OBE. Ambassador, Permanent Representative of Saint Lucia to the United Nations on Behalf of the Alliance of Small Island States (AOSIS) at the 14th Session of the Commission on Sustainable Development', www.un.org/esa/sustdev/csd/csd14/statements/stlucia_01may.pdf

Centre for Science and Environment (1998) 'Definitions of equal entitlements', Factsheet #5, Indian Centre for Science and Environment, www.cseindia.org/programme/geg/pdf/fact5.pdf

Government of the People's Republic of China (2004) 'Initial National Communication on Climate Change', http://unfccc.int/resource/docs/natc/chnnc1exsum.pdf

Other references

Jasanoff, S. and Wynne, B. (1998) 'Science and decision-making', in S. Rayner and E. L. Malone (eds) *Human Choice and Climate Change, Volume 1: The Societal Framework*, Battelle Press, Columbus, OH

Lakoff, G. (2002) *Moral Politics: How Liberals and Conservatives Think*, University of Chicago Press, Chicago, IL

United Nations Framework Convention on Climate Change (1992), http://unfccc.int/essential_background/convention/background/items/1349.php

2

The Many Faces of the Dispute

Faced with a vast number of arguments, facts and dimensions of climate change, we will find it helpful to group them or sequence them in ways that are meaningful in a quest to understand various elements of the global debate. As researchers have shown, our minds are not good at holding many unrelated pieces of data in memory. However, we are good at holding multiple bits of knowledge in chunks. We can, for instance, create higher-level categories and 'chunk' material into them. I might not be able to remember a list of randomized objects, but I can remember three items each in the categories 'animals', 'vegetables' and 'minerals'. Another way to make connections among a large number of items is to tell a story that includes all of them.

In this chapter I will attempt to do both of these at once. The ensuing discussion sorts climate change debaters by their role in climate change issues. Where do the arguments come from? Who are the people seeking general attention when they talk about climate change? And what are their purposes in studying climate change and making arguments about it? The answers to all of these questions involve the history – or, rather, the several histories – of the issue.

So to the story and the groups. I trace the backgrounds of the various participants in the climate change debate with a very broad brush. These participants include physical scientists, social scientists, economists (as a special case of social scientists), politicians and political analysts, and those who study ethics and culture. Perhaps it seems strange to be looking at different groups of scientists, rather than just 'scientists'. The reason for this choice is the difference in timing and orientation of each group's participation. In sorting these out, I will often be showing my tendency to discuss social science groups in greater detail, reflecting my interests and knowledge. The orientations of these various groups are important because they influence all the elements of an argument I talked about in the introductory chapter.

Scientists constitute perhaps the most important group – certainly in numbers of debaters. As Ulrich Beck, in his book *Risk Society* (1992), writes, science is at once the cause of the problem, the discoverer of the problem and the likely source of solutions. That is, scientists created or at least enabled the greenhouse gas emissions that are contributing to climate change, mostly via technologies that produce energy and industrial goods.[1] Scientists discovered the issue and assembled information on it. And scientists are providing candidate solutions, again mostly via new technologies that will emit less or no greenhouse gases. Scientists are thus central to the climate change problem and its resolution. Moreover, science encompasses many different perspectives – some would say at least as many as there are disciplines and sub-disciplines. This discussion will try to discern the major perspectives.

Different Scientific Paradigms

At first sight, climate change looks like a purely scientific affair, and purely physical science at that. It seems to be concerned mostly with abstract and abstruse knowledge, specialized into various scientific fields. The articles and reports by atmospheric and other physical scientists are full of research findings that may be gibberish to many: what happens at the tropopause, the increase of greenhouse gas concentrations in parts per million by volume, watts per metre squared of radiative forcing, atmospheric lifetimes, the carbon cycle and so on.

Much of the analysis of climate change has been undertaken as scientific research about emissions of (invisible) gases from human activities, the physico-chemical reactions that produce the greenhouse effect, the impacts of any changes on precipitation, evapotranspiration, crop yields, sea-level rise and other items measurable only by high-tech scientific instruments. Most of the scientific researchers involved agree that all the research is rife with uncertainties (although scientific results are right about the general trends) and that significant climate change happens slowly (although it's happening now). In February 2007 about 600 physical scientists published a consensus statement that human releases of greenhouse gases are causing at least part of the climate change that is occurring (see the quotation in Chapter 1); still, that assertion leaves plenty of room for dispute.

The viewpoint of physical scientists studying climate and climate change can be set in the context of other scientists studying large Earth processes, like plate tectonics and earthquakes, solar storms and electricity anomalies, and the origins of life and its evolution throughout the sweep of history. In each case, the large-scale processes are studied as intrinsically interesting more than as relevant to the human species. For example, articles on climate change in *Science* magazine are, more often than not, reporting research on the climates of past ages, with no reference to the present. I have talked to US climate scientists who say they took up studying climate change because it was the biggest problem around, which meant that they could continue to explore their interests in, for example, partial differential equations as used on the spherical Earth or large-scale computing processes. Several came to this problem from studies of nuclear proliferation, also a problem of global scope with strong atmospheric and environmental components. They were interested in scientific puzzles generally, in their own disciplinary matter secondarily and in climate change because it was – and is – an excellent puzzle and an opportunity to push disciplinary knowledge.

Much of the physical (or natural) science research has been conducted within a descriptive paradigm, as Steve Rayner and I discussed in our 1998 essay 'The challenge of climate change to the social sciences'. Descriptive researchers prefer to count, weigh and otherwise measure; thus material things (even if invisible) are usually the focus of study. This perspective typically deals with total amounts in relation to one another – like the masses and relative positions of tectonic plates or (in our case) the amounts of the gases in the atmosphere, global average (mean) temperature and ocean circulation patterns. This perspective lends itself to assessing the overall situation, the major ways in which different factors vary and global-level totals. What are the proportions of various gases in the atmosphere, measured in parts per million? How warm are the atmosphere and oceans, either overall (averages) or in various places and heights or depths? How many 'heat units' and how much fertilizer and water produce how many tonnes per hectare of a crop? These are the kinds of questions descriptive scientists investigate.

The scientific issues of climate change, seen in this way, are not necessarily concerned with the human implications of such change, nor of choices that could be made. So it's not surprising that the implications of climate change for human societies were studied only after the dimensions of the problem were seen more clearly. In a sense, economists and other social scientists were 'called in' to fill in data and knowledge gaps after physical scientists had outlined the physical dimensions of the issue.

For example, Charles Keeling, an atmospheric scientist, devised a way to measure carbon dioxide in the atmosphere. He positioned his device on Mauna Loa in Hawaii, and the results of these annual measurements (Figure 2.1) showed steady increases in the concentration of carbon dioxide in the atmosphere (in parts per million by volume, ppmv). When it became clear from the Keeling Curve that the atmospheric concentration of carbon dioxide was steadily increasing, it became interesting and important to measure how much of this carbon dioxide came from natural sources and how much from human sources – that is, what the contribution of human activities was to increased carbon dioxide in the atmosphere. Economists and engineers began to estimate carbon dioxide emissions, largely from the burning of fossil fuels (coal, oil and natural gas), and other scientists examined the natural sources of carbon dioxide that migrates to and from the atmosphere in processes such as plant growth and decay.

So physical scientists framed the climate change issue as a physics puzzle. And when social scientists took up the puzzle, they tended to take their framing from the physical scientists for the research that came to be the mainstream of climate science. Thus the social scientific research that most people see is subordinated to the physical science research, and relevant research related to societal causes of and responses to climate change is hardly seen at all.

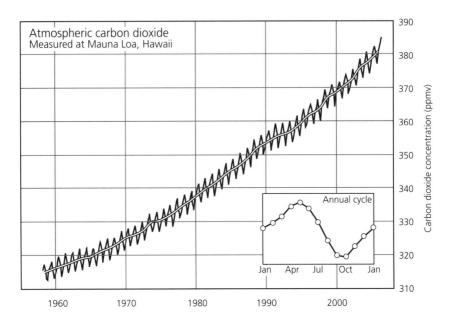

Figure 2.1 *The Keeling Curve, showing increasing proportions of carbon dioxide in the atmosphere*

In contrast to the descriptive paradigm, social scientific research is often conducted within an interpretive paradigm. Such research focuses on the meaning people ascribe to various aspects of their lives and on their cultural values. Studies are typically conducted at a relatively small scale, for example a village or institution. Interpretive research seeks insight into the nature of human experiences, how people perceive their worlds, what their interests are, how they filter or frame issues, and why they might decide that certain issues call for action.

Here's one example of how the difference manifests itself. Emissions of greenhouse gases drive the models that project climate change – and thus emissions are seen as quantities to be measured. Another way to analyse emissions, however, is as outcomes of human societal choices. The difference in the two framings is profound.

If scientists focus on descriptive research, such as how much carbon dioxide is released from various fuels and how much all the smokestack emissions add up to, emissions become something inevitable, a 'given'; thus climate change may be the inescapable product of inexorable human develop-ment. Emissions quantities may be manipulated in a model and the model can show reductions in quantities, but the model cannot tell how these reductions might be accomplished except through sweeping policy choices or price changes. (Often the trigger for change in an emissions model is a tax on carbon dioxide, a pure price signal.) But if, in contrast, emissions are seen primarily as resulting from human choices about how to produce energy and use land (the two largest sources), then that framing easily leads to a discussion of other choices that could be made. The first framing favours solutions that take energy demand as a given while developing alternative means of production. The second framing opens a broader framework for action that includes both supply and demand, from scaling back energy consumption to making choices that involve no-emissions energy (walking, doing things by hand, allowing sunlight to work and so on) to developing alternative means of production.

Different Histories

How did it happen that physical science framings came to dominate the debate? At least two broad-brush, capsule histories can be articulated about the relationship between the social and physical sciences in global climate change research.

One such history might start with mathematician/physicist Jean-Baptiste Fourier's 1824 suggestion that 'air traps heat, as if under a pane of glass' and keeps the Earth warm. This was probably the first description of the greenhouse effect by a scientist. Fourier's suggestion was followed by physicist/chemist Svante Arrhenius' identification of the so-called greenhouse effect (Arrhenius, 1896) along with his calculation of expected degrees of warming if the concentration of carbon dioxide in the atmosphere doubled. In the 20th century, modern computers allowed researchers to examine the physical and chemical processes by which carbon dioxide and other gases play a role in regulating the Earth's climate. With additional interest in modelling climate at a global scale, several large-scale research programmes developed general circulation models, or GCMs. These models and studies led to investigations into the economic-energy activities that result in greenhouse gas emissions. But only in the 1990s did the scientific research community finally arrive at the recognition of so-called 'human dimensions' as an important aspect of climate change research.

A second history might begin with philologist George Perkins Marsh's work *Man and Nature* (1864), which was subtitled *Or Physical Geography as Modified by Human Action*. Marsh began from a viewpoint that did not ignore people but recognized their role in altering the rest of Nature for their own purposes. We can follow that thought to the concept of the 'noösphere' (a biosphere organized by human activity), a term used by Vladimir Vernadsky and later by Pierre Teilhard de Chardin (see Teilhard de Chardin, 1955). According to Vernadsky (1945), the noösphere (from the Greek 'nous', meaning mind) is created at the point when, just as the inanimate geosphere had been transformed by biological life, the biosphere is transformed by human cognition.

This history would then highlight early contributions of social scientists to research in the field of climate and society that focused mainly on the ways people directly coped with the hazards of natural climatic extremes and with the indirect economic effects of climate. Despite mainstream social scientists' efforts to distinctly articulate the differences between social and physical science and to keep their distance from the latter, a handful of both types of scientists kept probing the nature of people's relationships with nature. Gradually, however (this version of history continues), mainstream science organizations such as the International Geosphere-Biosphere Program (IGBP), despite paying lip service to the importance of social science research, marginalized such research in add-on organizations (here we are back to 'human dimensions' programmes) or discounted social research studies as too localized. In a line of research largely separate from this history but relevant to social scientific research on climate change, political scientists who study international relations began to examine the negotiations before, during and after the UNFCCC was established.

These two capsule histories agree that social science research has come late to the climate change issue and principally as add-on programmes within larger programmes focused on the physical and chemical science aspects, from the atmosphere to agricultural outputs. The International Human Dimensions Program (IHDP) was launched in 1996 and exists on a shoestring budget relative to, for example, the IGBP. The US Climate Change Science Program devotes only a small fraction of its budget to decision-making issues and a miniscule amount to questions of socio-economic vulnerability and adaptive capacity.

Two developments have brought more social scientists into climate change research and debate in recent years, however. The first is a growing recognition that meaningful mitigation efforts are stalled. The most obvious example is the Kyoto Protocol, which commits countries to modest emissions reductions and was in limbo for eight years after it was formulated in 1997. Although it nominally came into force in 2005, the evidence so far indicates that, with very few exceptions, countries will not meet its goals. The second development is a resultant emphasis on adaptation strategies, coupled with a willingness to engage in more socially oriented research. Adaptation to climate change is inextricably bound up with governance and economic development issues that are already being examined in sustainable development, natural hazards and disasters, food security, and other research areas.

The social scientists Eugene Rosa and Thomas Dietz summarized the evolution of sociological research into climate change issues in a 1998 article. They discerned two broad types of research. One type sticks closely to data and observations. In this category is research that uses the constructs and findings of ecological science, integrating them with sociological insights to produce empirical results. For example, a line of research applies ecological concepts – such as the complex web of species interactions, disturbance and return time to equilibrium – in analysing socio-ecological systems; that is, how do human beings disturb the ecosystems they live in and how do those ecosystems (including the people in them) respond? Also in this category are analyses of the environment's role in economic stagnation and inequality as an instance of the workings of global capitalism. A second broad category focuses on how people make meaning from scientific and other types of knowledge, uncertainties in knowledge claims, and the social and political forces shaping scientific and public recognition of climate change as a problem. For example, broad surveys have shown how the public understands (or does not understand) climate change concepts and what priority they place on addressing the issue. Rosa and Dietz concluded by calling the late 1990s 'the incipient stage of our sociological understanding of [global climate change]'.

The history of scientists' involvement in climate change research would be incomplete without a discussion of the Intergovernmental Panel on Climate Change (IPCC). The IPCC, formed in 1989, has been a focal point for examining scientific research. By bringing together various scientific author teams, the IPCC has published four extensive assessments of relevant science. These assessments are not research in themselves, but rather summaries and evaluations of what research studies have said about a topic, a sort of state-of-the-science report. The IPCC was designed to insulate climate change science from broader international development issues. The IPCC has reflected a continuing tension between the modern scientific, technical conception of climate change and the increasingly messy ethical and political considerations.

Three working groups were formed in 1989: (1) science, (2) impacts and (3) response strategies. These working groups, which produce separate volumes and summaries as well as an overall Synthesis Report, have persisted through four assessment reports. From their subject areas, Working Group 1 should consist of physical and chemical scientists (and, because of the reliance on models, computer scientists), Working Group 2 of earth systems scientists with participation from economists, and Working Group 3 of social scientists of all kinds. In fact, the participation of social scientists in the entire process of the First Assessment Report was summarized as 'lamentable' (Redclift, 1992). Working Group 1, looking at atmospheric chemistry, climatology and ecology, achieved a remarkable level of consensus and is widely recognized as representing the highest quality international scientific collaboration. An example of their results is shown in Figure 2.2 – comparative contributions of various greenhouse gases, complete with uncertainties shown by vertical lines above and below the bars. The other two working group volumes proved highly controversial where they touched on issues such as local and aggregated projected damages of climate change, because they raised issues of economic and social inequality, forms of governance, and human rights. Demographic issues, for instance, were not discussed (beyond the use of population projections).

However, as the debate changes from 'Is it real?' to 'What to do?', social science research and perspectives are more and more in evidence. Research formerly sidelined is now recognized as relevant; much of this has been conducted using an interpretive approach.

In climate change research, interpretive studies have addressed the framing of the problem as well as issues of stakeholder involvement, sociocultural values, the nature and production of knowledge, and policy implementation

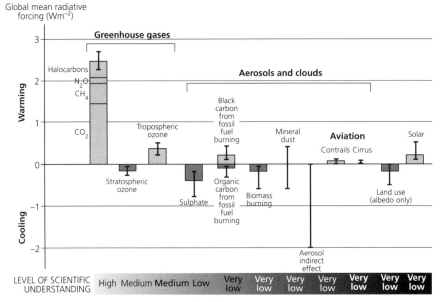

Note: The height of a bar indicates a best estimate of the forcing, and the accompanying vertical line a likely range of values. Where no bar is present the vertical line only indicates the range in best estimates with no likelihood.
Source: IPCC (2007)

Figure 2.2 *Physical science research results showing the relative contributions of gases to increasing global warming and other climate changes for the year 2000 compared to 1750*

(research and development investments, technology selection and diffusion, and so on). Cultural anthropologists and sociologists have examined the claims and worldviews of government, science and indigenous people in environmental disputes. In contrast to macro-level theory about international relations, political scientists have studied the ways in which individual actors form networks and epistemic communities. Whole literatures focus on behavioural changes in energy and technology use, as well as how technologies come to be adopted. Social scientists investigate how real-world public policymakers and industry decision-makers decide what to do, as opposed to idealized models of people who only respond to price signals; and historical studies demonstrate societal responses to climate changes in the past. Geographers and urban and land-use planners analyse the ways people use the resources of the places they live in and the impact of that use both now and in the future. And social research into climate change is increasingly coupled with considerations of sustainable development (Cohen et al, 1998; Herbert and Robinson, 2000); this research has always emphasized governance and culture.

Social scientists use many conceptual tools. One example is a matrix that scientists use to analyse two or three values (perhaps 'high', 'medium' and 'low') of two or three variables. Or, like Figure 2.3, a visualization can be a

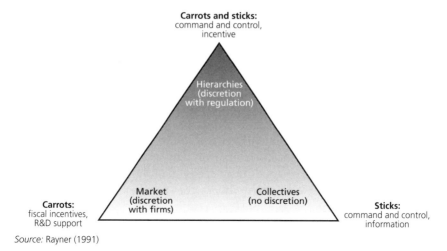

Source: Rayner (1991)

Figure 2.3 *Policy preferences of cultural types*

kind of 'idea map', in this case showing what kinds of policies people with different cultural values might favour.

At this point I want to step back to discuss the special case of economics in the climate change debate. As discussed earlier, economic scientists and analysts have formed the principal bridge between physical science studies of the climate and climate change impacts on Earth systems, and human causes and response options. Quantitative studies of emissions associated with energy production came first from economics-based models; these studies fed into climate studies that attempted to simulate climate change via an increase in carbon dioxide emissions. The first climate change studies used a doubling of the carbon dioxide concentration in the atmosphere as a way to try to gauge what the effect of that increase would be – on both the climate and, by extension, climate-dependent systems, the most obvious being agriculture. Such studies almost immediately raised the question of whether that kind of increased level is likely. To find out the answer to that question requires determining what the sources and quantities of carbon dioxide emissions are and what the rate of increase has been and is projected to be in the future from these various sources.

The social science most in evidence in all four assessments to date (1990, 1995, 2001 and 2007) was economics. Economists addressed very specific questions, starting in the first report: calculation of emissions from human activities and damage functions and mitigation costs, presented as totals at the global or large regional level. This large-scale analysis fed into climate model calculations – and also helped to avoid the issue of differentiated impacts on people in various places. In later reports, such analyses have been improved and extended, for example by including greenhouse gases other than carbon dioxide and adding regional detail about the sources of emissions and the costs of reducing them.

Economic approaches are the most widely applied social science tools in contemporary industrialized society and have contributed much to our understanding of what climate change could mean – and especially what efforts to reduce greenhouse gas emissions could mean – for global and country-level societies. Broadly considered, economic activity is the source of greenhouse gas emissions, since economic activities include everything that people do in their livelihoods and in the production of goods for their use. More narrowly, however, economics focuses on markets and the prices of things. Its central paradigm is the individual consumer, a person who works for wages and buys goods in a rational way: those goods fulfil needs and how much they cost. This 'rational actor' (in principle all of us) always goes for the lowest priced goods that fulfil his or her basic needs. If potatoes cost less than rice, he or she would buy potatoes; if taking the bus to work is less expensive than driving but takes the same amount of time, she or he would take the bus. These two examples show that this paradigm leaves a lot out: cultural or taste preferences (for rice over potatoes, for example) and side benefits (such as the comfort and convenience of one's own car). So the 'rational actor' is not a realistic model for many of us. Our decisions may be influenced by economic considerations, but almost always other factors enter in too. Moreover, sometimes people find reasons to purchase the most expensive product on the market. They make consumer decisions about an array of goods and services based on many factors, perhaps including price, but perhaps not. However, the usual economic analysis leaves out all factors except price.

Another highly relevant assumption in economics is that growth is good; indeed, stagnation and recession are problematic for both societies as wholes and economists. Therefore, following from this assumption, producing or using less of something should be avoided, unless there are better products available. Producers should be producing more and better goods, incomes should be increasing, and consumers should be spending more. This assumption, that growth is good, is not entirely realistic either; just ask someone who has been 'downsized' as corporations grow by acquiring other companies.

Still, at a highly aggregated level, such as a country or the world, quantifying and analysing markets can be quite useful. In the case of climate change, economists have used a standard economic measure – gross domestic product (GDP) – to measure both human welfare and the cost (in percentage of GDP) of efforts like reducing greenhouse gas emissions. Other measures are labour productivity, the costs of goods and services, the rate of technological change, and the extent of trade. These measures all relate to economic growth (or lack of it), and all would be affected by the kinds of impacts climate change would bring.

Economists have also elaborated a framework in which to think about and model the problem. This framework is called the IPAT equation:

Impact = Population × Affluence × Technology

This equation-like statement, roughly translated, says that the impact of climate change can be calculated from knowing the total population, their affluence and the technologies they use. From this statement comes the Kaya identity (Kaya, 1990), a variant on it:

$$CO_2 \; Emissions = \; Population \times (GDP/Population) \times (Energy/GDP) \times (CO_2/Energy)$$

This is the key to much of the analysis of carbon dioxide emissions. What it says is that carbon dioxide emissions are equal to the number of people multiplied by GDP per capita, by the energy used per dollar of GDP and by the carbon dioxide released by some unit of energy. The calculation therefore requires information about population, GDP, energy generated in some unit (for example exajoules) and the emissions from one unit of energy.

Using this identity, economists have developed quantitative tools, called integrated assessment models (IAMs), for studying the whole issue, from emissions through climate changes to impacts. Figure 2.4 shows a typical framework for such models, with emissions generated in one box (lower left) causing changes in the atmosphere and climate (top two boxes), with impacts on the Earth and its systems (lower right).

When used as a framework of relationships, the IPAT framework and its kin have been and continue to be useful. However, when analysts consider each element as a separate stressor, IPAT becomes a distorted picture (MacKellar et

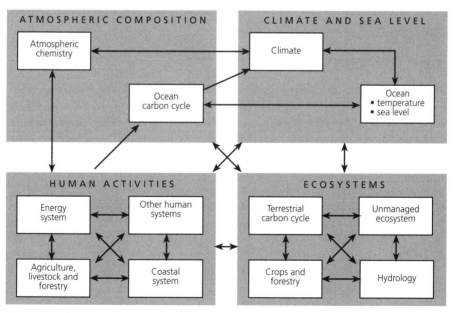

Source: www.climatescience.gov

Figure 2.4 *Integrated assessment modelling framework*

al, 1998; Chertow, 2001). Those who blame economic growth or population growth for climate change miss their interrelationship. Economic growth is obviously tied to population growth, but the relationship of the two and the implications for continued population growth can be read in different ways. We could picture a world in which more people continue to increase their demands for the goods of an industrialized society without considering environmental costs, adversely affecting the environment, including the climate. Conversely, we could picture a world in which more people used their increased wealth to protect the environment and lessen both climate change and its effects. Of course, a smaller, prosperous population could either emit great quantities of greenhouse gases or decide that a better environment, including no further human-made climate change, was a high priority and thus reduce emissions. So the number of people in the world in itself does not indicate a specific level of carbon dioxide emissions.

This brief, interwoven history of scientists' participation in the climate change issue from its discovery to its debate in non-scientific arenas demonstrates the differences between what we might call 'ideal' science – with objective results derived from carefully designed experiments – and science as a community of scholars who have different backgrounds and operate within different paradigms. Scientists themselves are different; different questions interest individuals and groups, and they use different tools. Even isolating groups such as physical scientists, social scientists and economists does not reflect major differences within each group. Moreover, beyond the research communities, the theoretically sharp line between science and the other elements of society becomes blurry when scientific findings seem to have implications for politics and societal wellbeing.

Other Voices in the Debate

Physical scientists, economists and other social scientists have brought disciplinary framings and disciplinary knowledge to the climate change issue. Scientists have doubtless played essential roles in getting the climate debate going and keeping it going. But they are by no means holding the debate by themselves. Other participants are playing major roles in the climate change debate. The post-World War II history of environmental issues led to an expectation that governments, having been informed by scientists that a problem existed, would do something about it. And the history of political involvement must include the history of environmental activism broadly, then specific environmentalist efforts focused on climate change and policymakers, principally at the country level.

Contemporary environmentalism, beginning with the 1962 publication of Rachel Carson's *Silent Spring* (or, according to some historians of the movement, with Earth Day in 1970), is characterized by activists working to reduce or eliminate the pollutions of the nuclear age and industrialism (MacDonald, 2003; Yearley, 1991). Although a number of deadly incidents had been blamed on the effects of fossil fuel use – for example the 'killer fogs' in London (1948 and 1952), a devastating oil spill in Santa Barbara (1969), and smog in Los Angeles and other cities – the requirements of economic progress had taken precedence over the need to curtail pollution until this time. Indeed, chemical companies attacked Carson personally as hysterical and extremist, and car companies vigorously resisted a specific requirement to recycle engine emissions.

But Carson's book, other evidence that people could see and their strong reactions to it, and some political leadership in the unlikely form of President Richard Nixon helped to bring environmental concerns to the fore in the US. (See Shabecoff, 1993, for a good account of the US environmental movement.) Banning the pesticide DDT and nuclear weapons, cleaning up the air and water, strictly controlling the use of toxic materials, limiting lumbering, halting the needless killing of animals such as whales, and holding industries accountable for polluting the environment were goals of activist organizations and individuals beginning in the 1960s. Tactics ranged from media campaigns to lawsuits to hugging trees, lying in front of bulldozers and interfering with whaling vessels. Beginning in the 1960s, the Natural Resources Defense Council, the Environmental Defense Fund (1966), EarthFirst!, the League of Conservation Voters, Greenpeace and many others – local, national and international – lobbied, demonstrated, sued firms and governments, and generally pushed hard to stop harmful practices and preserve environmental resources and places. In other parts of the world, people tried to stop the encroachments of industry and modern markets and to protect their traditional land uses and cultural practices. A famous example of this is the Chipko movement in India, which had notable successes in 1973 and 1980. Women hugged trees and otherwise interposed their bodies between the trees and workers trying to cut them down.

The 1970s saw a plethora of environmental laws passed in the US: the National Environmental Protection Act; the Federal Insecticide, Fungicide and Rodenticide Act (FIFRA); and laws to regulate water pollution, coastal zone management, safe drinking water, toxic substances, resources conservation management and clean air. President Nixon created the Council on Environmental Quality and the Environmental Protection Agency. The focus was on command-and-control legislation, however, and the results of this approach often fell short of expectations. Furthermore, land use was not addressed; land-use planning that accounts for environmental issues is inadequate at the local level and hotly contested on a regional scale and remains politically impossible at the national level, despite the appeals of such well-known manifestos as Aldo Leopold's *The Land Ethic* (1949). In Britain and Europe, Green political parties formed, traditional political parties were anxious to be seen as 'green', and industrial firms set about developing at least the appearance of environmental concern. In so-called Third World countries, environmentalism became part of the struggle against the culture- and nature-destroying aspects of industrialization.

The activist wave was succeeded by a 'Third Wave', in which environmentalists attempted to work within political processes and with corporations to set up laws, regulations and agreements that would be environment-friendly. Environmentalist organizations developed teams that included lawyers, lobbyists, scientists, economists, organizers, fundraisers, publicists and political operatives so they could effectively influence government decisions. In the US, these groups became more pragmatic and focused on working 'within the system' to achieve environmentally favourable goals. The new pragmatists also recognized that more complex problems, such as climate change, were emerging and that industry groups were devoting greater resources to oppose them. The national organizations became adept at mass communication techniques as well as grass roots, door-to-door efforts.

Many conservation and activist organizations became Third-Wavers, devising schemes for market-based policies and negotiating directly with industry. Environmental organizations have become more numerous and more like their opponents in style and tactics, although protests, direct action and 'witnessing' are still in evidence.

Climate change non-governmental organizations (NGOs) emerged as the issue did – first as additional issues within the scope of larger environmentalist organizations, then as stand-alone organizations perhaps focused on providing scientific information, merging interests among smaller groups or advising governments. For example, the Mountain Forum was formed to share information about the implications of climate change for high-elevation environments and to represent otherwise isolated and sparsely populated regions in the political activities of the UNFCCC. The London-based Foundation for International Environmental Law and Development (FIELD) wrote position statements and acted for the Association of Small Island States (AOSIS) in international negotiations. By the time of the Earth Summit in 1992, more than 1400 NGOs registered as participants in that conference.

With this recent history in mind, scientists and environmentalists might be forgiven for thinking that they were identifying a problem that surely would be taken up and addressed in policies. And in the late 1980s and early 1990s this seemed to be happening.

Voices of policymakers joined the conversation about climate change. In the wake of the discovery of the ozone hole and the 1987 Montreal Protocol to reduce emissions of CFCs, global climate change appeared on the policy agendas of many countries, including the US. Concern was then heightened by the very hot summer of 1988, when droughts and heatwaves seemed to announce the advent of global warming. Jim Hanson, a scientist at the US National Aeronautics and Space Administration (NASA) who had been prominent in the discovery of the ozone hole, testified in the US Congress that there was a 'strong cause-and-effect relationship' between greenhouse gas emissions and the warming experienced in that summer. In addition, international scientific organizations such as the World Meteorological Organization (WMO) and the United Nations Environment Programme (UNEP) were sending messages that climate change needed to be taken seriously, reinforced in that pivotal year, 1988, by the World Conference on the Changing Atmosphere in Toronto, Canada. The conference included both scientists and decision-makers, and the group concluded that carbon dioxide emissions should be reduced, proposing a 20 per cent reduction by 2005 as an initial goal, along with an international framework convention to protect the atmosphere. That was also the year that several national governments asked the WMO and UNEP to establish the Intergovernmental Panel on Climate Change (IPCC), which came into being the next year.

Study and discussion led to the Earth Summit (official name: the United Nations Conference on Environment and Development, or UNCED) in 1992, held in Rio de Janeiro (so it's also referred to as the Rio Conference or just Rio), at which the nations of the world signed up to the UNFCCC. There was something for just about everyone in the UNFCCC: affirmations about the importance of the Earth's environment for everybody; promised reductions in emissions of greenhouse gases, obviously the responsibility of the big emitters, the rich nations; and promised assistance for less industrialized nations.

But there was plenty of strategic ambiguity too. The UNFCCC did not specify *how* countries were to deal with the problems of greenhouse gas emissions, economic growth, safeguarding adaptation, technology transfer, and so on. It was up to subsequent Conferences of the Parties to work out these 'details'. The UNFCCC kicked off the process, but the job of the politicians was far from over. Although it set out principles about fairness and equity, the responsibilities of the industrialized countries *vis-à-vis* the less industrialized countries, balance of impacts on the environment and the economy, and so on, these are precisely the issues that politicians are still debating.

The process of developing an international convention with more specific agreements to follow allows participants to agree where they can and to defer the issues they disagree on. This is precisely what happened with the UNFCCC. Although the longer, slower process of developing specific agreements under the UNFCCC can theoretically help to build trust and consensus among disparate parties, the same process may also be open to delays and blockages (intended or unintended).

Just as scientists choose study areas and make arguments in the context of their scientific communities and their own interests, so environmentalists act within a framework of principles that give meaning and force to their affiliations, and policymakers analyse and negotiate within a context of political communities and specialized policy areas.

Environmentalists may come to the issue of climate change from a prior concern with another environmental problem (say nuclear waste or air pollution) or a whole-world issue such as globalization, poverty, or food and water scarcities. They may have a history of involvement with social movements or be galvanized into action by this specific issue, because they know someone who is interested in it or because they see a leader who inspires them. Thus, they bring to the climate change issue prior concerns and affiliations, which influence the kinds of arguments they make in the debate.

The voices of policymakers on the subject of climate change vary in many dimensions: personal interest and knowledge, function in the government, network contacts with scientists and other policymakers on the subject, constraints given by national-level policies and priorities, and resources available for participation in negotiations and policy development. Like many scientists and environmentalists, many of them come to the issue of climate change from other issues, perhaps environmental issues, perhaps not. They may have an understanding of the scientific knowledge, but more often they take a purely political approach to the issues.

All the groups discussed here are composed of people who are simultaneously individuals, members of families and affinity groups, members of work categories, workers at specific places, and citizens of localities and countries. Each person thus brings a plurality of identities and social ties, and in discussing issues he or she will attempt to strengthen existing identities and ties as well as form new ones. The principal tools used include nonverbal and verbal communication: they wear certain types of clothes, consume specific goods and so on – and they talk. They talk to define themselves, establish relationships with others and come to agreement with others about issues that seem to them important.

Before we venture into this world of talk about climate change, the next chapter examines a possible strong parallel between the climate change and globalization debates.

Note

1 This is not exactly true, as historians of the so-called Industrial Revolution make clear. Often technology development led the way, with scientists trying to explain why the technologies worked.

References

Arrhenius, S. (1896) 'On the influence of carbonic acid in the air upon the temperature of the ground', *Philosophical Magazine*, vol 41, pp237–276

Beck, U. (1992) *Risk Society: Toward a New Modernity*, trans. M. Ritter, Sage, London

Carson, R. (1962) *Silent Spring*, Houghton-Mifflin, Boston, MA

Cohen, S., Demeritt, D., Robinson, J. and Rothman, D. (1998) 'Climate change and sustainable development: Towards dialogue', *Global Environmental Change*, vol 8, no 4, pp341–371

Chertow, M. R. (2001) 'The IPAT equation and its variants; Changing views of technology and environmental impact', *Journal of Industrial Ecology*, vol 4, no 4, pp13–29, http://mitpress.mit.edu/journals/pdf/jiec_4_4_13_0.pdf

Herbert, D. and Robinson, J. (2000) 'Integrating climate change and sustainable development', in M. Munasinghe and R. Swart (eds) *Climate Change and Its Linkages with Development, Equity, and Sustainability*, IPCC and WMO, Geneva

Kaya, Y. (1990) 'Impact of carbon dioxide emission control on GNP growth: Interpretation of proposed scenarios', presented to the IPCC Energy and Industry Subgroup, Response Strategies Working Group, Paris (mimeo)

Leopold, A. (1949) *A Sand County Almanac*, 1977 reprint, Oxford University Press, New York

MacDonald, G. (2003) 'Environment: evolution of a concept', *Journal of Environment & Development*, vol 12, pp151–176

MacKellar, L., Lutz, W., McMichael, A. J. and Suhrke, A. (1998) 'Population and health', in S. Rayner and E. L. Malone (eds) *Human Choice and Climate Change. Volume 1: The Societal Context*, Battelle Press, Columbus, OH

Marsh, G. P. (1864) *Man and Nature, or Physical Geography as Modified by Human Action*, 1965 reprint, Belknap Press, Cambridge, MA

Rayner, S. (1991) 'A cultural perspective on the structure and implementation of global environmental agreements', *Evaluation Review*, vol 15, no 1, pp75–102

Rayner, S. and Malone, E. L. (1998) 'The challenge of climate change to the social sciences', in S. Rayner and E. L. Malone (eds) *Human Choice and Climate Change, Volume 4: What Have We Learned?*, Battelle Press, Columbus, OH

Redclift, M. (1992) 'Sustainable development and global environmental change: implications of a changing agenda', *Global Environmental Change: Human and Policy Dimensions*, vol 1, pp32–42

Rosa, E. and Dietz, T. (1998) 'Climate change and society: Speculation, construction and scientific investigation', *International Sociology*, vol 13, pp421–455

Shabecoff, P. (1993) *A Fierce Green Fire: The American Environmental Movement*, Hill and Wang, New York

Teilhard de Chardin, P. (1955) *The Phenomenon of Man*, 1961 reprint, Harper & Row, New York

Vernadsky, V. I. (1945) 'The Biosphere and the Noösphere', *American Scientist*, January, pp1–12

Yearley, S. (1991) *The Green Case: A Sociology of Environmental Issues, Arguments and Politics*, Harper Collins Academic, London

3

Climate Change:
Part of Globalization?

'The world is too much with us', as William Wordsworth wrote in the 19th century, and today global problems seem to be crowding in on us more than ever. Issues that we collect under the term 'globalization' include international trade and financial transactions, instantaneous and seemingly open exchange of information and messages, infectious diseases, terrorism, and environmental problems – including climate change.

If climate change is more or less one item on a globalization laundry list, then the debate is really all about globalization and should be analysed as such. In order to determine if this is the case, in this chapter I will examine both globalization and climate change using the same framework. (See Malone, 2003, for an earlier version of this framework.) Overlap is, of course, expected, but if the analysis is essentially the same, we can safely conclude that the issues have so much in common that they should be studied as one.

Roland Robertson and Anthony Giddens, who focus on globalization as an issue, talk about it as the closer relationships between things in time and space. There are connections at a distance, 'in such a way', says Giddens (1990, p64), 'that local happenings are shaped by events occurring many miles away and vice versa'. Robertson (1992, p100) adds the connections concerned with scale: that global-level conditions immediately affect local places and what occurs in a community may quickly be taken up by the world at large. In the case of climate change, we could apply this definition by saying that the global climate is present in my neighbourhood, and the carbon dioxide I emit locally from heating my house and driving my car affects the global climate.

That's OK in general, but we need more than generalities to discover how 'globalization' and 'climate change' relate to one another. Is climate change just another category within globalization, is it the other way around or are they quite different? In discussions of one issue, associating it with another issue may bring some unwanted baggage along, clouding or distorting the original issue. So it's worthwhile to analyse each term and think about what the two concepts have in common and where they are different. This has implications for both the content and the conduct of arguments in the climate change debate.

The two issues have spawned two different literatures; each refers to the other concept, however. Globalization theorists invoke climate change as part of a vague set of environmental issues. Climate change analysts, in their turn, both blame globalization for environmental problems and attempt to mobilize support for environmental causes by appealing to global citizenship and responsibility in slogans such as 'Love Your Mother' (Earth). Although globalization has enabled climate change to become a point of debate and climate change has contributed to the definition of globalization, neither concept necessarily contains the other. They may look more like a Venn diagram, with both unique and shared features.

The concepts differ in their emphases on cultural, economic and political aspects. Climate change has strong ties to the cultural aspects and issues of globalization (especially in the domain of science, considered as an element of culture), but more local economic and political issues play large roles in the debates around the sources, consequences and possible policies of climate change. Globalization's usual realm deals more with economics and trade than with science and the environment, although there are obvious (and not-so-obvious) overlaps. Both globalization and climate change have strong implications for politics and policymaking at the international level, and here they may have much in common.

The concepts can also be usefully compared in how they express the relationship between the global and the local. Three views are common:

1   The global and the local are in competition and sometimes conflict (as when, for example, groups engage in violent protests against multinational companies or World Trade Organization agreements).
2   The global dominates the local (as when, for example, an international fast-food chain puts local restaurants out of business).
3   Hybrids or mixtures are born of global and national and/or local elements (as when, for example, so-called world music is blended with local rhythms to create new dances and melodies).

Theorizing Globalization

Two dimensions – cultural/economic/political aspects and the relationship of global and local – provide a framework for looking at each concept, then comparing them. For globalization, the framework looks like Table 3.1, with examples at each intersection.

The economic dimension of globalization

Economics dominates many discussions of globalization (see, for example, Wallerstein, 1974 and 1983; Piore and Sabel, 1984; Harvey, 1990). Prominent topics include multinational firms, the global marketplace, rules of trade and

Table 3.1 *Globalization dimensions*

	Economic	Political	Cultural
Global/local conflict	Attempts to nationalize multi-national industry	Resistance to WTO, terrorism	Separatism of native groups
Global domination	Flexible specialization instead of mass production	Standard forms of government	McDonaldization
Hybrids and mixes	Western goods sold in bazaars	Terrorist groups, 'global village'	Blended musical forms

trade balances. Nations, locales and groups may resist global economic flows, may come to be dominated by them or may 'domesticate' them in various ways.

Places themselves, as well as people, may seem to be resistant to global efforts to remake them. Many stories have been told, for instance, of international development projects that have left virtually no imprint on the targeted countries or locales. Buildings sit unused; technology breaks down and is left to rust; national debts mount instead of being reduced. Some countries have shown no positive results after decades of foreign investment. Other resistors of note are the protest groups who show up at every World Trade Organization (WTO) meeting and native populations who block various forms of land-use change.

Global industries may, on the other hand, dominate local places. The demands of the global marketplace dictate what the small factory makes or what the farmers grow. Large chain stores may be able to undercut the prices of local businesses and drive them out.

Another form of global economic domination comes out of producers' responses to the diverse demands of the global market, which will not accept mass-produced, identical goods. One response is to develop a decentralized structure and technologies that can produce a range of products for different customers (Piore and Sabel, 1984). A good example is speciality steels that have different constituents and characteristics (hardness, brittleness and so on) depending on their uses, but that can all be made at one plant. Of course, flexible specialization and responsiveness to the global market result in workers who have less and less job security, both because of fluctuating demands and because factories may move to places where labour or capital costs are lower (Beck et al, 1994; Beck, 1999). And local places may not be able to protect such workers (but are left with the burden of supporting them when jobs are eliminated).

The third broad alternative is a hybrid or mix of the global and the local. Products of multinational companies, such as jeans and sneakers, are sold in age-old local bazaars, for instance (Abu-Lughod, 1997). In another example, the book *Golden Arches East* (Watson, 1997) disputes the usual thesis that McDonald's takes over the market everywhere it builds restaurants. The book tells how McDonald's restaurants in East Asia are put to different uses, depending on the city. In Beijing family feasts are popular, while in Hong Kong single women appreciate the safety and cleanliness, and students gather to do homework in Seoul. Each global, lookalike restaurant has also adapted its menu to local tastes. Reversing the process, ethnic groups find that their traditional handiworks may be sold all over the world – with a tweak here and there to appeal to a global consumer group.

The political dimension of globalization

In addition to global markets and flows of goods, globalization involves political structures and relationships. These are often seen as competing or even in open conflict (politics being, after all, a dimension concerned with power). Dominance is also a major power theme, with global forms of government being implemented in various countries and the US working to maintain its position of superpower after the end of the Cold War. Finally, the popular concept of the global village shows how local cultures maintain their individuality while drawing on global elements of culture.

Globalization is often seen politically in opposition to nationalism – and both may be seen as the forces of stability versus disruptive groups often lumped together as terrorists but also including marauding militias. Thomas Friedman, in *The Lexus and the Olive Tree* (1999), views this contrast as an intertwined political and economic dichotomy.

Social and political theorists may not accept the concept of global domination because they assume that the highest-level actors are countries. If countries have the final say-so in matters that affect them, then no international authority really exists; there is a kind of anarchy in the international sphere, and no global authority can gain legitimacy in governing multiple countries. Even allowing that countries can negotiate agreements that they then adhere to, the topics of those agreements may just be items on the international agenda – and secondary items at best, after the perennial items of war, security and national self-interest (see, for example, Mann, 1993).

Against the idea that the nation state is the ultimate source of power, at least some of that power has been increasingly ceded to international organizations (global domination in Table 3.1), including the United Nations, the European Union and the WTO, by governments that increasingly look alike despite working very differently (Thomas and Meyer, 1984; Meyer, 1999). A typical government may have some kind of constitution, a legislature, a president or prime minister, and various agencies or ministries (including an environmental ministry), but its political structure may be run by party bosses who pay little attention to the established structures. Countries are parties to various treaties, even though they may neglect or flout the provisions of these treaties.

Political groups may be hybrids, partly local and partly global. For instance, some terrorist groups rely on local loyalties and ethnicities, yet use the communication tools and weapons of the larger world around them. In a more benign example, the global village concept seeks to integrate appreciation of diversity and mutual caring among the far-flung places of the world.

The cultural dimension of globalization

The cultural dimension has received less attention than the economic and political dimensions, but the three types of interaction among globalization and localism are evident here also.

Global and local cultures may compete, even come into conflict. Forcible efforts to open up areas to tourism or economic activity (say forest clearing) may be violently resisted by indigenous people (Friedman, 1990). Global values or campaigns may seek to eradicate such local cultural practices as clitorectomies and other mutilations, repression of women in various ways, or harvesting natural resources – only to be fought by people who seek to protect their ways of life.

Or globalization may mean that all culture becomes dominated by the global, a melding of local cultures (Appadurai, 1996). This implies cultural imperialism, American culture being the most frequent nominee (Galtung, 1997; Hall, 1997). In another form of global domination, global culture may mean the organization or structure of many cultures; although cultural products differ, the manner of producing, distributing and marketing them may become similar for every culture (Garcia Canclini, 1995; Smith, 1990). A standard production-and-consumption system, part economics and part culture, is used by the US to export McDonaldization, credit cards, Disney Worlds, 'eatertainment' establishments and shopping malls (Ritzer, 2000; Ritzer and Malone, 2000).

The third alternative is that global culture may simply be one additional culture, to be examined alongside national and local cultures, with no particular hierarchy involved (there are hybrids and mixes); one can pick and choose from global, national and local products and identities (Robertson, 1992; Featherstone and Lash, 1995). Modern transportation and communication enable people to see places around the world as easily as places next door to them – and to experience different cultures, environments and conditions (even – or maybe especially – war and famine) via print and electronic media. 'Cosmopolitans', people who take on roles in many cultures (unlike the 'locals' who want to stay at home wherever they go), help to provide coherence to the world culture (Hannerz, 1990 and 1997).

The global and the local may be experienced side by side. On the one hand, developing countries contribute more equally to global hybrids, such as in the melding of Western rock music and Bedouin 'dancing horse' patterns (Pieterse, 1995; Abu-Lughod, 1997). On the other hand, developed niches occur in many, mostly un-modern places around the globe, for example Tunis, with its Gucci and couture sweatshops and its modern Census Office. Globalization in this view defines a space in which the world's cultures rub shoulders and generate new meanings and understandings. It is possible to discuss Americanization, Europeanization, Japanization – and even Brazilianization (Featherstone and Lash, 1995).

Contributions of Theorists to Understanding Globalization

Globalization theorists have explored a wide range of possible social relations resulting from contemporary processes and products of globalization (including the possibility that globalization is not unique in history, nor so pervasive as is usually thought – see Hirst, 1997; Henwood, 1999).

The economic analyses allow us to see (and perhaps counter) the implications of a global economy, including the advantages of free trade, information flows and international cooperation – but also the disadvantages to workers of flexible specialization (for example, uncertain, intermittent work and greater mechanization), the inequalities of global trade, and the continuing domination of a few national or regional economies.

In the political dimension, as nation states continue to be established, they use the established state forms whether or not their history and culture allow these forms to be successful; furthermore, poor and new states struggle for (or against) the 'benefits' of economic development. The politically oriented insights of globalization theory help us to understand these processes and (hopefully) to see ways of improving global wellbeing. Also, globalization theories add to explanations of global social movements such as those concerned with the environment, feminism and implications of 'free' world trade; in order to be successful, such social movements must espouse valid transnational (global) principles yet relate them to what's happening in each locale.

In the cultural dimension, globalization theories provide descriptions and insights about how people's processes of forming their identities are changing. Instead of roots in family and community, a person is exposed – for better and worse – to other cultures and ways of being, including people and settings that are truly international. A person may feel at home almost anywhere or may try to eat, speak and generally live the same way no matter where he or she is. These approaches to lifestyle are polar responses to globalization. Then there are people who combine the traditional and the global, such as *les sapeurs* in the People's Republic of Congo, who buy Paris fashions to gain local status (Friedman, 1990). Or people may constitute their identities by connecting to global-level groups on the basis of, for example, gender, profession, interest in humankind (perhaps in social movements) or economic group (Robertson, 1992). Yet another possibility is that individual identities can be formed out of bits and pieces of national and ethnic cultures in a kind of mixture (Hall, 1997). The many options may result in societies where nobody can count on any kind of shared values or practices, although in practice people do make assumptions about just these cultural traits.

After this very compressed look at the main threads of globalization analysis, we now turn to an analysis of climate change and compare it to the analysis of globalization.

Approaches to Theorizing Climate Change

Global climate change – or 'global warming', as it is often called[1] – is simultaneously an exemplar of globalization and a type of universalization that transcends globalization. It may be the result of capitalism/consumerism (an economic dimension), modernity (a political/governance dimension) or science itself (a cultural dimension).

Counter to the view that climate change is just one manifestation of globalization is the view that climate change has raised issues ignored in discussions of globalization. The new regimes and institutions constructed around the issue of climate change are extensive, reaching from science to policy to grassroots movements and raising hotly debated questions about whose knowledge is used and who speaks for Nature.

After the beginning of the Cold War, the US sought national security partly through international scientific and political cooperation. The stage was thus set for political, economic and cultural globalization (led, in the 'free world', by the US) and, in the case we are looking at, for scientific investigations of global problems, including climate change.

Scientists studied the link between carbon dioxide (and other radiatively active gases) and changes in the Earth's climate, helped by improved and expanded measurements and advances in computational power. The post-war push for international scientific cooperation resulted in a global network of atmospheric observing and measurement stations under the newly formed World Meteorological Organization (WMO). In 1958, the International Geophysical Year, Keeling began measuring the level of carbon dioxide in the atmosphere over Mauna Loa (as discussed in Chapter 2); this record clearly showed rising levels. Meanwhile, computer models of the climate system were being developed, first of the atmosphere, then of the ocean. Research increased during the 1980s and 1990s, on both national and international scales.

Most discussions of globalization that include the environment as a topic include climate change in a list of global environmental issues, such as the thinning ozone layer, decreasing biodiversity, sustainable development, pollution and over-fishing in the oceans, and acid rain. These became part of the international environmental movement and a new social structure, the 'network society' (the term is from Manuel Castells's 1997 three-volume work *The Information Age*). Themes of the environmental movement include a love–hate attitude towards science and technology (as simultaneously the source of many environmental problems and the source of information about them), the need to control space and time, an emphasis on local places, and a view of species and matter as a global whole.

Table 3.2 *Climate change dimensions*

	Economic	Political	Cultural
Global/local conflict	Free trade agreements vs. national environmental standards	Modern bureaucracy clashes with national traditions, e.g. Chipko movement	Concern for global climate vs. issues of responsibility for the problem and equity between nations
Global domination	Capitalist world system mires some nations in poverty and vulnerability to climate change	Transnational social movements, standard state forms, 'ecological modernization'	Western science and scientists define the problem and solutions
Hybrids and mixes	Emissions trading systems, ecological economics, sustainability	Green parties seek to reduce emissions	'Local knowledge' added to scientific knowledge

Climate change too can be analysed in the three-by-three matrix used in the discussion of globalization (Table 3.2).

A comparison of the tables for globalization and climate change (enlarged in scope to include other global environmental problems) shows some similarities but more differences. A brief cell-by-cell discussion shows not just changes in emphases but the new issues and arguments that arise around climate change:

- **Economic global/local conflict** Here the issues are very alike – attempts to set global rules and standards are met with resistance from firms and industries seeking rules that maximize their profits.
- **Economic global domination** Instead of globalization's focus on how industries create global markets and disadvantage workers, the argument in the climate change debate is about economic inequality among nations, industrialized countries emitting the lion's share of emissions while poorer and already-vulnerable countries will be most negatively affected by climate change.
- **Economic hybrids and mixes** For globalization analysts, this means goods from one place showing up in all sorts of places and situations; for climate change, hybridization means extending tools, such as cost–benefit analysis, that did not include environmental factors to treat the environment as part of a market or markets – quite different from the globalization emphasis.
- **Political global/local conflict** Globalization and climate change are similar in their foci on large governmental decisions being resisted by small groups, for example terrorists in the first case and indigenous people and their resource use in the second.
- **Political global domination** Globalization studies examine how governmental structures increasingly look alike, whereas climate change analyses

look beyond national governments to other forms of governance, including transnational social movements and global standards for addressing climate and other global changes.

- **Political hybrids and mixes** Both globalization and climate change literatures focus on local groups, for instance native peoples (relevant to globalization) and green parties (relevant to climate change), who adopt global goals and tools such as the internet and seek international support.
- **Cultural global/local conflict** Globalization studies examine the conflicts between global businesses/cultures and native groups with long, non-global traditions and practices. Climate change research focuses on issues of global environmental citizenship versus more local interests such as jobs.
- **Cultural global domination** In the globalization realm, the dominant global culture is American, including ways of eating, entertainment and transportation. Climate change analysis, however, focuses on the dominance of Western science in defining the problem and its solutions.
- **Cultural hybrids and mixes** Films, 'folk' products and musical forms draw from all parts of the globalized world. In climate change studies, again the focus is on science, here coupled with various forms of local knowledge about the climate in specific places.

But in fact the table structure that adequately reflects the scope of the globalization literature proves to be not very well suited to the scope of the arguments in the climate change debate. We could rename the right-hand column 'Science', which would help, but the table would still be missing the environmental dimension, which does not easily divide into the global–local relationships defined in the table structure.

Economic globalization and climate change

Issues not raised under globalization include questions about the tendency of the capitalist production system to favour here-and-now benefits over delayed but more uncertain benefits (the so-called high discount rate) and to produce both goods and environmental degradation.

One view is that the world cannot have the good life without the bad environment (Beck, 1986; Giddens, 1991; Yearley, 1996; Sachs, 2000). The production of environmental bads is a direct function of the capitalist need to use 'free' resources in order to accumulate capital (Saurin, 1996; Wallerstein, 1999). Efforts to 'value' the environment (for example the 'polluter pays principle') are steadfastly resisted or, when resistance is futile, such costs are passed on to consumers. In fact, goes one argument, industries need free natural resources so much that, if companies had to pay for environmental resources, they couldn't do business (Wallerstein, 1999). Governments can and are buying time by such strategies as shipping wastes to a politically weaker South and constraining growth in newly industrializing countries. But eventually there are only three options:

1   Force businesses to pay all costs, resulting in drastically reduced profits;
2   Make governments pay, resulting in large tax increases and probably a profit squeeze from reduced consumption; or
3   Do nothing and face various ecocatastrophes.

In this discussion, it is difficult to separate climate change from other environmental issues, especially those considered 'global'.

Meanwhile, unchecked economic globalization will continue to exacerbate (if it does not cause) problems such as climate change, indoor pollution, household and industrial wastes, water availability, poor air quality, and extinction of species.

But some economists see this issue as simply a failure to price natural resources – in other words, a market failure, albeit one little discussed in the globalization literature (Daly, 1992; Redclift, 2000). Ecological economics and ecological modernization advocate setting prices on natural resources and seeking to develop technologies that will be less polluting, less environmentally degrading, more efficient and so on. Ecological modernization posits the potential for controlled, sustainable growth that can yield both economic prosperity and no environmental damage (as expressed in the slogans 'win–win', 'win–win–win', the 'triple bottom line' and 'pollution prevention pays').

Political globalization and climate change

Global political issues under the label of 'modernity' have been held up as the all-purpose cause of climate change. The modern political system reinforces globalization and allows unchecked greenhouse gas emissions, especially from energy production and land-use change, two primary mechanisms of modernization.

So far, this argument mostly tracks globalization arguments, but it becomes the bridge to discussions about sustainable development, which is not a standard globalization topic. The governance accompaniment to 'sustainable development', which focuses on changing the present system, is ecological modernization. In this view, a great mistake of modernity was to define the environment (Nature) as external to human societies and their production/consumption systems. People have assumed that they are exempt from natural constraints; that is, people are not subject to the laws of Nature in the same way that other species are, but instead can control the rest of Nature through technologies. The alternative to this view encompasses human beings and their natural environment together. One reaction to this insight is 'demodernization theory', an aspiration to a green society of small communities that live in harmony with Nature and the natural climate. Another is ecological modernization, coupled with ecological economics, as discussed above. Both have strong implications for modern governance. In essence, today's societies can repair this mistake of modernity with more modernity, including much better management of environmental resources as well as societies. In climate change, ecological modernization is the theory that underpins proposed policies like emissions trading schemes and tax breaks for renewable energy industries and technologies.

Specific climate change examples focus on the inequalities of the world system, now intensified by climate change. Industrialized countries are responsible for the historic emissions that are the cause of the steep rise in atmospheric greenhouse gases. But the resulting climate change impacts will largely be felt in the tropics, where most of the poor, formerly colonized and non-industrialized countries lie (Agarwal and Narain, 1991). A proposed global transition to 'green' fuels and technologies in order to mitigate climate change may similarly and disproportionately disadvantage poor groups and nations (Boehmer-Christiansen, 2003). For example, as poor countries fall into debt, they are forced to sell the products of 'free' natural resources, thus exposing themselves to harm from both economic globalization and climate change (Sachs, 2000; O'Brien and Leichenko, 2000; O'Brien et al, 2004).

With regard to the environment, countries have achieved international agreements codified in treaties and conventions, but implementation has fallen far short of what is envisioned in, for example, the UNFCCC. This may be a crisis of authority, since organizations such as the United Nations lack legitimacy necessary for implementation, monitoring and enforcement. Furthermore, international agreements depend upon individual nation-states to implement the terms of the agreement. However, the nation-state may in fact be too small to effectively meet global environmental challenges and too big to implement appropriate policies at local levels (Redclift, 2000). Noting that global is *not* a synonym for international, political scientists and others (for example Saurin, 1996; Dovers, 2001; Young, 2008) call for new global institutions capable of dealing with the ordering processes involved in the scale, spread, complexity and dynamics of global environmental changes.

Cultural (scientific) globalization and climate change

Science is the principal cultural element involved in climate change issues. It may seem odd to lump science with cultural topics such as fashion, film and fast food, but science has become an essential way in which the world, but especially the world's industrialized countries, makes cultural meaning out of the environment and societies we live in, just as fashion, film and food do. Moreover, science is associated with larger issues of knowledge production and use.

As such, science plays a special role in global climate change related to the problem itself and to the nature of scientific knowledge and its uses. Science has constructed the problem and moreover constructed it as a global problem with at least some human causes in the emissions of so-called greenhouse gases. As a scientific issue, climate change was 'discovered' by advances in scientific understanding and methodology and computational capacity, as outlined earlier (Beck, 1986). Moreover, scientific/technological methods are among the most often proposed ways of addressing climate change.

Of course, scientific methods and conclusions have been the subject of intense debate, even when the overall trends and causes are agreed on. Perhaps the measurement of greenhouse gases does not represent the global atmosphere; there is uncertainty about emissions of greenhouse gases, particularly from land-use changes; the models, because they are global models, cannot be verified (what could they be compared to?) and may neglect important processes; and the current warming trend may be unrelated to human activities and more dependent upon sunspot cycles, for example (Edwards, 2001; Norton and Suppe, 2001). The issues of 'globalizing science' mostly relate to generalizing from localized experiments or data (Jasanoff and Wynne, 1998).

Climate change is global in its very nature, unlike some other scientific issues with far-ranging relevance. Pasteur's work in germ theory, for example, had global relevance, because wherever contagious disease is present his constructs can be applied. But Pasteur did not need to collect data on a global system like the climate system but rather to replicate his experiments and hygienic practices at multiple locations. In contrast, the global climate system must be considered as a whole. Storms in the Pacific Ocean drive much of the weather that much of the world experiences. Emissions of carbon dioxide go into the stocks of the whole atmosphere. And so on.

Science is indispensable in discussions about global climate change. Indeed, scientific research has made it possible for people to think of the globe as a symbol of a common humanity. The picture of the Earth from space (the 'big blue marble') has evoked descriptions of its fragility, its limited resources and human dependence. Associated images of Spaceship Earth and Gaia (the sense of the whole Earth as a living being) join earlier images of Mother Earth with powerful, global messages to 'protect' the Earth and 'Love your Mother'. These are global images and cultural constructions that provide the appropriate settings for global climate change discussions, all enabled by science.

On the ground, however, where inequalities in costs and benefits are continually observed, questions arise about the accuracy and value of scientific knowledge and how that knowledge will be used along with other kinds of knowledge, such as traditional farming methods, land uses and governance patterns. Prescriptions from industrialized nations, such as advice to less industrialized nations on 'clean development' and technology-dependent 'solutions', are likely to face scepticism. Calls for development assistance without the strings of capitalist institutions may well fall on deaf ears. The current state of negotiations on climate change seem to confirm the theory that there is anarchy in the international sphere (as discussed earlier), with self-interests dictating outcomes rather than a recognition that cooperation may bring advantages for all.

Globalization and Climate Change: More Heat than Light?

What is the relationship between globalization and climate change? Economic, political and cultural globalizations are deeply implicated as the causes of climate change and our knowledge about it. In each dimension, analysts have suggested both 'more' and 'less' to meet the challenges of climate change – that is, we should either promote globalization as the best way of protecting the environment or dismantle the global economy and allow localities to control their own resources. In the economic sphere, capitalism may either be expanded to account for the input costs of and damages to the environment or be superseded by another economic system, one friendlier to the environment. In the political sphere, the alternatives proposed include *more* government that extends itself to manage the environment along with social systems or retreat to locally sustainable governments. In the cultural sphere, science needs to either specify methods to mitigate and to adapt to more fully characterized climate changes or to lose its hubris and make space for local knowledges and for moral and ethical approaches to the issues raised by global climate change.

Climate change certainly brings up many economic, political and cultural/scientific issues, some of which can be debated under the heading of globalization. Climate change globalizes the environment by specifying the connections among what happens in specific places and the whole climate system. Non-governmental environmentalist organizations and institutions have gone a certain distance down the globalization path by including multiple kinds of knowledge and viewpoints. An international organization, the Intergovernmental Panel on Climate Change, although dominated by industrialized-nation scientists, has come to some conclusions that are not in the interests of their nations. The supranational United Nations Environment and Development Programmes have had modest success in providing assistance to poor nations which are not well adapted to current climate variability and which face further problems under long-term climate change. Still, industrialized nations are not actually overhauling their energy systems, and there is little indication of systematic planning for adaptations that will be necessary.

The proliferation of theories and analyses in both globalization and climate change reflects the emerging nature of both areas of social scientific thought. Activities and 'flows' are changing too rapidly to be satisfactorily categorized and mapped. Moreover, there are no clear advantages to one form of action, since all phenomena are multifaceted, with bundled positive, neutral and negative characteristics. For example, global policy on climate change could benefit all nations on average but leave specific groups mired in poverty and at risk of climate change impacts. However, local initiatives, while empowering stakeholders and taking advantage of local knowledge, may be limited in resources and subject to countervailing activities elsewhere (as when forests are spared in one place but cut down in another). Non-governmental organizations can work across national boundaries on sustainable development programmes but be undermined by local and national governments. Green communities reduce their emissions of greenhouse gases and serve as models for other communities, but they may also be marginalized and powerless to effect change in larger political spheres.

If this is an incoherent assemblage of activities, it is also a vibrant and plurivocal one. Climate change forums have provided venues for many voices to be heard on a global stage, and climate change concerns have galvanized scientific research, policy debate and local action. Innovations multiply in the form of supranational environmental institutions, market-based environmental regulatory instruments and the rise of engagement from a global civil society.

Still, there are important contradictions to be sorted out. An overwhelming majority of people want a less degraded environment, but seemingly at the same time everyone wants more goods and energy to improve the world's standard of living. Governments pay lip service to improving or protecting the environment, but back off from the expense and change that would result from many environmental policies, so that few effective ones have been enacted *and* implemented. International institutions or non-governmental organizations may be more matched to the scale and complexity of climate change, but to date they have not been able to make other actors compromise, concede or act.

Although it is tempting to resign oneself to expect the reproduction of existing power structures in the debate about climate change, history contains examples of large social changes against the expectations of the powerful; social revolutions that resulted in democratic governments constitute an obvious example, but peaceful changes, for example in medicine and sanitation, also occur. No change occurs, however, without arguments, discussion and debate. So we will turn in the next chapter to talking about talk.

Note

1 Most physical scientists who perform climate change research think 'global warming' a reductionist term, since climate change includes a multitude of possible changes, up to and including increased frequency and intensity of storms, prolonged drought in places, and the disruption of the Atlantic Ocean's 'conveyor belt', the Gulf Stream.

References

Abu-Lughod, J. (1997) 'Going beyond the global babble', in A. D. King (ed) *Culture, Globalization and the World-System: Contemporary Conditions for the Representation of Identity*, University of Minnesota Press, Minneapolis, MN

Agarwal, A. and Narain, S. (1991) 'Global warming in an unequal world: A case of environmental colonialism', Centre for Science and Environment, New Delhi

Appadurai, A. (1996) *Modernity at Large: Cultural Dimensions of Globalization*, vol 1, D. Gaonkar and B. Lee (eds) University of Minnesota Press, Minneapolis, MN

Ausabel, J. H. (1991) 'Does climate still matter?', *Nature*, vol 350, pp649–652

Barber, B. (1995) *Jihad vs. McWorld*, Times Books, New York

Beck, U. (1986) *Risk Society: Toward a New Modernity*, 1992 reprint, M. Ritter (trans), Sage, London

Beck, U. (1999) *World Risk Society*, Polity Press, Cambridge, UK

Beck, U., Giddens, A. and Lash, S. (1994) *Reflexive Modernization: Politics, Tradition and Aesthetics in the Modern Social Order*, Stanford University Press, Stanford, CA

Boehmer-Christiansen, S. (2003) 'Science, equity, and the war against carbon', *Science, Technology & Human Values*, vol 28, pp69–92

Castells, M. (1997) *The Power of Identity. Volume II of The Information Age: Economy, Society and Culture*, Blackwell, Malden, MA

Catton, W. R. Jr and Dunlap, R. E. (1980) 'A new sociological paradigm for post-exuberant sociology', *American Behavioral Scientist*, vol 24, pp14–47

Cobb, C., Halstead, T. and Rowe, J. (1995) *The Genuine Progress Indicator: Summary of Data and Methodology*, Redefining Progress, Oakland, CA

Daly, H. (1992) *Steady-State Economics*, Earthscan, London

Davis, M. (2001) *Late Victorian Holocausts: El Nino and the Making of the Third World*, Verso, New York

Dovers, S. (2001) 'Institutions for sustainability', Australian National University, http://een.anu.edu.au

Easterly, W. (2001) *The Elusive Quest for Growth: Economists' Adventures and Misadventures in the Tropics*, MIT Press, Cambridge, MA

Edwards, P. N. (2001) 'Representing the global atmosphere: Computer models, data, and knowledge about climate change', in C. A. Miller and P. N. Edwards (eds) *Changing the Atmosphere: Expert Knowledge and Environmental Governance*, MIT Press, Cambridge, MA

Featherstone, M. (1990) *Global Culture: Nationalism, Globalization and Modernity*, Sage, London

Featherstone, M. and Lash, S. (1995) 'Globalization, modernity and the spatialization of social theory: An introduction', in M. Featherstone, S. Lash and R. Robertson (eds) *Global Modernities*, Sage, London

Friedman, J. (1990) 'Being in the world: Globalization and localization', in M. Featherstone (ed) *Global Culture: Nationalism, Globalization and Modernity*, Sage, London

Friedman, T. (1999) *The Lexus and the Olive Tree*, Farrar, Straus and Giroux, New York

Galtung, J. (1997) 'On the social costs of modernization: Social disintegration, atomie/anomie and social development', in H. de Alcántara (ed) *Social Futures, Global Visions*, Blackwell, Oxford, UK

Garcia Canclini, N. (1995) *Hybrid Cultures: Strategies for Entering and Leaving Modernity*, University of Minnesota Press, Minneapolis, MN

Giddens, A. (1990) *The Consequences of Modernity*, Polity Press, Cambridge, UK

Giddens, A. (1991) *Modernity and Self-Identity: Self and Society in the Late Modern Age*, Stanford University Press, Stanford, CA

Guston, D. H. (2001) 'Boundary organizations in environmental policy and science: An introduction', *Science, Technology & Human Values*, vol 26, pp399–408

Haas, P. M. (1992) 'Knowledge, power and international policy coordination', *International Organization*, vol 46, no 1

Hall, S. (1997) 'The local and the global: Globalization and ethnicity', in A. D. King (ed) *Culture, Globalization and the World-System: Contemporary Conditions for the Representation of Identity*, University of Minnesota Press, Minneapolis, MN

Hannerz, U. (1990) 'Cosmopolitans and locals in world culture', in M. Featherstone (ed) *Global Culture: Nationalism, Globalization and Modernity*, Sage, London

Hannerz, U. (1997) 'Scenarios for peripheral cultures', in A. D. King (ed) *Culture, Globalization and the World-System: Contemporary Conditions for the Representation of Identity*, University of Minnesota Press, Minneapolis, MN

Harvey, D. (1990) *The Condition of Postmodernity: An Enquiry into the Origins of Cultural Change*, Blackwell, Malden, MA

Held, D., McGrew, A., Goldblatt, D. and Perraton, J. (1999) *Global Transformations: Politics, Economics and Culture*, Stanford University Press, Stanford, CA

Henwood, D. (1999) 'What is globalization anyway?', *ZNet Commentary*, vol 1999, www.zmag.org/zspace/commentaries/262

Hirst, P. (1997) 'The global economy – Myths and realities', *International Affairs*, vol 73, pp409–425

Hobsbaum, E. (1992) *Nations and Nationalism since 1780: Programme, Myth, Reality*, Cambridge University Press, New York

Jasanoff, S. and Wynne, B., with Buttel, F. H., Charvolin, F., Edwards, P. N., Elzinga, A., Haas, P. M., Kwa, C., Lambright, W. H., Lynch, M. and Miller, C. A. (1998) 'Science and decisionmaking', in S. Rayner and E. L. Malone (eds) *Human Choice and Climate Change, Volume 1: The Societal Framework*, Battelle Press, Columbus, OH

Kaplan, R. D. (1994) 'The coming anarchy', *The Atlantic Monthly*, February, pp44–76

Malone, E. 'Climate change and globalization', *Social Thought and Research*, vol 25, no 1–2, pp143–173

Mann, M. (1993) 'Nation-states in Europe and other continents: Diversifying, developing, not dying', *Daedalus*, vol 122, pp115–140

Meyer, J. W. (1999) 'The changing cultural content of the nation-state: A world society perspective', in G. Steinmetz (ed) *State/Culture: State-Formation after the Cultural Turn*, Cornell University Press, Ithaca, NY

Miller, C. A. and Edwards, P. N. (2001) 'Introduction: The globalization of climate science and climate politics', in C. A. Miller and P. N. Edwards (eds) *Changing the Atmosphere: Expert Knowledge and Environmental Governance*, MIT Press, Cambridge, MA

Mol, A. P. J. (2000) 'Globalization and environment: Between apocalypse-blindness and ecological modernization', in G. Spaargaren, A. P. J. Mol and F. H. Buttel (eds) *Environment and Global Modernity*, Sage, London

Norton, S. D. and Suppe, F. (2001) 'Why atmospheric modeling is good science', in C. A. Miller and P. N. Edwards (eds) *Changing the Atmosphere: Expert Knowledge and Environmental Governance*, MIT Press, Cambridge, MA

O'Brien, K. L. and Leichenko, R. M. (2000) 'Double exposure: Assessing the impacts of climate change within the context of economic globalization', *Global Environmental Change: Human and Policy Dimensions*, vol 10, pp221–232

O'Brien, K. L., Leichenko, R. M., Kelkar, U., Venema, H., Aandahl, G., Tompkins, H., Javed, A., Bhadwal, S., Barg, S., Nygaard, L. and West, J. (2004) 'Mapping vulnerability to multiple stressors: Climate change and globalization in India', *Global Environmental Change*, vol 14, pp303–313

Paterson, M. (1996) 'IR theory: Neorealism, neoinstitutionalism and the Climate Change Convention', in J. Vogler and M. F. Imber (eds) *The Environment and International Relations*, Global Environmental Change Series, Routledge, London

Pielke, R. Jr, Prins, G., Rayner, S. and Sarewitz, D. (2007) 'Lifting the taboo on adaptation', *Nature*, vol 445, pp597–598

Pieterse, J. N. (1995) 'Globalization as hybridization', in M. Featherstone, S. Lash and R. Robertson (eds) *Global Modernities*, Sage, London

Piore, M. J. and Sabel, C. F. (1984) *The Second Industrial Divide: Possibilities for Prosperity*, Basic Books, New York

Redclift, M. (2000) 'Environmental social theory for a globalizing world economy', in G. Spaargaren, A. P. J. Mol and F. H. Buttel (eds) *Environment and Global Modernity*, Sage, London

Ritzer, G. (2000) *The McDonaldization of Society: New Century Edition*, Pine Forge Press, Thousand Oaks, CA

Ritzer, G. and Malone, E. L. (2000) 'Globalization theory: Lessons from the exportation of McDonaldization and the New Means of Consumption', *American Studies*, vol 41, pp97–118

Robertson, R. (1992) *Globalization: Social Theory and Global Culture*, Sage, London

Robertson, R. (1995) 'Glocalization: Time-space and homogeneity-heterogeneity', in M. Featherstone, S. Lash and R. Robertson (eds) *Global Modernities*, Sage, London

Robertson, R. (2001) 'Globalization theory 2000+: Major problematics', in G. Ritzer and B. Smart (eds) *Handbook of Social Theory*, Sage, London

Sachs, W. (2000) *Globalization and Sustainability*, Heinrich Boll Foundation, Berlin

Saurin, J. (1996) 'International relations, social ecology and the globalisation of environmental change', in J. Vogler and M. F. Imber (eds) *The Environment and International Relations, Global Environmental Change Series*, Routledge, London

Scott, J. (1998) *Seeing Like a State*, Yale University Press, New Haven, CN

Smith, A. D. (1990) 'Towards a global culture?', in M. Featherstone (ed) *Global Culture: Nationalism, Globalization and Modernity*, Sage, London

Solow, R. M. (1991) 'Sustainability: An economist's perspective: J. Seeward Jonson Lecture', Woods Hole Oceanographic Institution, Woods Hole, MA

Sonnenfeld, D. A. and Mol, A. P. J. (2002) 'Globalization and the transformation of environmental governance: An introduction', *American Behavioral Scientist*, vol 45, pp1318–1339

Spaargaren, G. (2000) 'Ecological modernization theory and the changing discourse on environment and modernity', in G. Spaargaren, A. P. J. Mol and F. H. Buttel (eds) *Environment and Global Modernity*, Sage, London

Thomas, G. M. and Meyer, J. W. (1984) 'The expansion of the state', *American Sociological Review*, vol 10, pp461–482

Tobin, J. and Nordhaus, W. (1972) 'Is growth obsolete?', in *Fiftieth Anniversary Colloquium V*, National Bureau of Economic Research, Columbia University Press, New York, NY

Vogler, J. and Imber, M. F. (eds) (1996) *The Environment and International Relations*, Routledge, London

Wallerstein, I. (1974) *The Modern World-System*, Academic Press, New York

Wallerstein, I. (1983) *Historical Capitalism, with Capitalist Civilization*, Verso, London

Wallerstein, I. (1999) 'Ecology and the capitalist costs of production: No exit', in W. Goldfrank, D. Goodman and A. Szasz (eds) *Ecology and the World-System, Studies in the Political Economy of the World-System*, Greenwood Press, Westport, CN

Watson, J. (ed) (1997) *Golden Arches East: McDonald's in East Asia*, Stanford University Press, Stanford, CA

Yearley, S. (1996) *Sociology, Environmentalism, Globalization*, Sage, London

Yohe, G., Cantor, R. et al (1998) 'Economic analysis', in S. Rayner and E. L. Malone (eds) *Human Choice and Climate Change, Volume 3: The Tools of Policy Analysis*, Battelle Press, Columbus, OH

Young, O. (2008) *Institutions and Environmental Change: Principal Findings, Applications, and Research Frontiers*, MIT Press, Cambridge, MA

4

Arguments:
Agreeing and Disagreeing

In the previous chapter, I analysed globalization and climate change to see if the climate change debate is really about globalization – if the two issues are essentially the same. Despite some elements in common, the climate change issue has several distinct features that set it apart as an issue to be analysed on its own. So this chapter begins an in-depth analysis of the wide-ranging global conversation we are having about climate change.

The possibility that human activities have become so large in scale that they are affecting the global climate system has become a matter of extensive debate; the debate itself and the arguments made in it is the focus of this book. Intentional human attempts to affect the weather have a long history, of course: people have prayed or danced or sacrificed or performed other rituals to persuade the gods to send rain, fair weather or whatever conditions might facilitate human endeavours. What is different in the present situation is that a scientific basis exists to believe that human beings, without intending to, may be affecting the climate and that climate change may have negative consequences. The debate, then, is about whether human emissions of so-called greenhouse gases are affecting the climate and, if so, what people should do to address the potential for climate change.

The first task that anyone who makes an argument faces is that of convincing the audience that there is something requiring their attention, something arising from outside themselves and suddenly confronting them, like the urgency that arises in military battles or political situations such as the Cuban Missile Crisis (Bitzer, 1968). But the person who makes that argument may be at least partially creating that urgency by the very act of arguing that the evidence presents a problem that people should take notice of and do something about (Vatz, 1973). The evidence of climate change (rising carbon dioxide concentrations, emissions of greenhouse gases and so on) became the basis for a scientific argument about how climate is or may be affected by emissions of carbon dioxide and other greenhouse gases to the atmosphere. Thus scientists were the first to construct climate change as a problem. This scientific argument is an especially important element, because, unlike battle-fields or photos of missile silos, the evidence of climate change is a highly artificial construct (although we have learned that photos may not be the evidence they seem to be either). The evidence that carbon dioxide concentrations in the atmosphere are rising comes from complex scientific instrument measurements, represented by a graphic curve familiar to climate scientists (see Chapter 2) but not empirically verifiable by a non-scientist, as an oil spill or smog is. Projections of climate change are presented as graphs, charts and other visualizations of computerized simulations.

The scientific basis for potential climate change caused by human beings has many people worried, but others remain unconvinced. That is, some accept the argument that climate change is something to worry about and argue for (and against) particular actions to respond to the threat, while for those who do not accept climate change as a problem, the framing of the topic continues in scholarly and political debates.

Within the ranks of those who believe human-caused climate change is a problem, research attention in recent years has begun to focus on the processes involved in constructing climate change as a socio-environmental 'problem', creating evidence of it and attempting to develop solutions at the global level. After the initial agreement (the UN Framework Convention on Climate Change, UNFCCC, came into force in 1994), progress has been slow at best, and the Framework Convention is seemingly at an impasse. The number of policy proposals is legion, but even the modest emissions reductions agreed to in the 1997 Kyoto Protocol will probably not come to pass, and the protocol itself came into force only in 2005 and without the US. Argumentative fissures have appeared, not only in the arguments associated with so-called 'developed' versus 'developing' countries, but also within these groups of countries.

How to Examine the Arguments?

Given the seeming inability of people to come to agreement about what (if anything) to do about the prospect of climate change, should the world's societies continue to try to find a path forward? In order to answer this question, we should examine the arguments people are making. An analysis of the arguments in the debate *as arguments* should shed some light on the potential for agreement. If there are bases for agreement, they should exist in the arguments themselves – in the definition of the situation, or in one or more of the premises, or in proposals made. Even conceding the well-known phenomenon that people do not always say what they mean or believe, we can also be sure that opponents in the debate will ferret out hidden motivations and arguments. So if we examine a wide enough range of arguments, we should be able to capture most of the real arguments. Perhaps differences in the characteristics of the speakers or perceived biases form the bases for disagreement, rather than the content of the premises or conclusions. Furthermore, a closer look at the arguments in the debate may yield insights about how to build on areas of agreement and gain adherence to one or more proposals for action.

To conduct this analysis, I start with the tools of rhetorical analysis. For the ancient Greeks, rhetoric was the art of persuasive speaking and writing; today, the term is largely used in a negative sense, meaning fine-sounding but empty phrases, either meaning nothing or attempting to trick the audience: 'mere' rhetoric. The difference between what Aristotle meant and the usual meaning today is one of purpose: for Aristotle, rhetoric was aimed at establishing the truth. People debated so as to arrive at facts or principles they could agree were true. Today, without the mooring of truth-seeking, the term has lost its lustre; nevertheless, I will use the term as the correct one to describe the ways in which people try to persuade others.

Rhetoric has been a field of study and an academic discipline since those ancient times. Features of persuasive speaking and writing – how an argument is put together – have been almost endlessly categorized. My contention is that the most basic of these categorization schemes, the one presented in the first chapter of this book, provides a structured way not only to examine the arguments in the climate change debate, but also to compare them, element by element, with a view towards gaining a deeper understanding of the points of agreement and disagreement.

In *The Art of Rhetoric*, Aristotle set up three categories of appeal in an argument: the character of the speaker (ethos), the appeal to the emotions of the audience (pathos) and the claims of the matter itself (logos). Who is the speaker and why should others listen to him or her? How does the subject connect with the values the audience holds dear? And why is the subject itself important? Each person who constructs an argument must wrestle with each of these three dimensions. Furthermore, each speaker in a debate constructs an argument based on a worldview that is presumably shared among speaker and hearers; otherwise, the argument would be unconvincing or, indeed, unintelligible.

The study of persuasive speaking and writing eventually split into two camps. One camp focused on formal structures of arguments, from syllogisms to symbols used. Everything is named and catalogued, from major premises to warrants, from metaphors to enthymemes[1] (Perelman and Ohlbrechts-Tyteca, 1969). The second camp focused on affective aspects of arguments – as dramas, for example, enacted for the benefit of audiences, or as energized by the various desires of participants (Burke, 1989; Ling, 1989; Wells, 1996).

But, of course, this is a false dichotomy. A successful argument is both structured well – has a logic that others can agree with – and makes sense as a kind of impassioned narrative. Conversely, an argument may be criticized on the grounds either that it isn't logical or doesn't hang together, or that the whole thing just doesn't make sense and is not something anyone cares about.

And here we are back to the elements of an argument discussed in Chapter 1 as we thought about families deciding what to do on vacations. Let's review this briefly, then extend the discussion to focus *how* arguments work (or don't):

- *Varying authorities of the debaters*: How much authority is claimed by or granted to a speaker (or writer, as the case may be). Bases for authority include age, status (professional or other), experience, control of resources, economic or military power, alliances, knowledge, and moral principles.
- *Degree to which the content matters to participants*: A debater may not care about the outcome of the debate sufficiently to make a strong argument, may care about only one or a few points rather than the whole issue, or be very passionate about everything. The degree of emotional investment may convince others that a proposal should or should not be adopted. It is also quite possible that passionate advocacy will backfire.
- *Acceptance of the evidence*: Reasons why the claims and proposals should be agreed to by the others in the debate. These may consist of facts, logic, appeals to known preferences, attempts to point out the moral or ethical dimensions, what happened previously, or organizational or personal characteristics.
- *Worldview*: Assumptions about how the world works and how societies function (and should function). Examples include the world as a place run by a benevolent, caretaking God; people as stewards of the Earth and caretakers of each other; or the world as a place where people compete for resources, power and wealth.
- *Acceptability of a proposal*: Recommended actions (or no action). Even when other elements of a debate may be hotly contested, participants may be able to offer proposals for action that can be agreed to by most or all other debaters. The arguments for a particular proposal may be based on intrinsic qualities of the proposal or on extrinsic factors.

The first step in examining the arguments about climate change will be to identify these factors in each of the major arguments; this is the subject matter of the next chapter. Interesting in itself for the insights gained about how people are talking to one another, this first-step analysis will lead to a second step. Having identified the factors, we can then compare each factor across all the arguments to find areas where there seems to be agreement or disagreement. This second-step analysis, detailed in Chapter 6, will provide a basis for building on existing agreements to move the conversation forward.

How do a whole argument and all its factors work to convince people who hear or read it? In discussing this topic, I will borrow freely from such rhetoricians and theorists as J. L. Austin (1962), Jürgen Habermas (1984 and 1987), Chaim Perelman and Lucie Olbrechts-Tyteca (1969), Stephen Toulmin (1958), Susan G. Wells (1996), and Jeanne Fahnestock (Fahnestock and Secor, 1993) – a few of the many scholars who focus on rhetoric and arguments.

The first point to note at the outset is that all participants in a debate agree about *something*. If I say the sky is green and you say it is blue, we agree that there is a sky. If the children want to go to the beach and the parents want to go to the mountains, they agree that they should go somewhere. The interesting aspects of a debate are identifying what participants agree about and analysing the degree of agreement.

Second is that all statements are also acts – that is, a speaker is always seeking to have an effect by making statements. The effect may be as life-changing as young people enlisting in the army and going to war, but more likely the speaker is simply trying to establish a social connection that will be favourable to him or her.

A third point (an extension of the second) is that speech acts are oriented towards mutual understanding between a speaker and listener (or writer and reader). This understanding may establish and renew interpersonal relations, represent states and events, and express the speaker's experience (roughly equivalent to Aristotelian pathos, logos and ethos). But in actual situations, this orientation towards understanding may be completely frustrated or distorted by various factors, including personal and contextual characteristics.

This mutual understanding is facilitated if the speaker or writer can conjure up a receptive audience. This receptive audience, the person or persons ostensibly addressed, may be very vague, a kind of universal audience, which consists of all people everywhere – or, at least, all adults who, if they under-stand the reasons given in the argument, would have to accept the conclusions. More than in most debates, participants in the climate change debate address the universal audience – sometimes grandly specified as humankind or all travellers on Spaceship Earth, sometimes the implied audience for scientific 'discoveries' (in other words everyone who is convinced by scientific arguments and evidence). So the appeal may be not to specific people, but to all fellow global citizens.

Fourth, speech acts claim to be valid and can be judged on the basis of whether they are morally correct, factually true and subjectively sincere. Thus, if a scientist shows data about the probability of risk from exposure to a toxic chemical, he or she is making a claim about the truth of the state-ments. Because the scientist knows that such statements can be contested, he or she frames the statements to be acceptable to the audience. Similarly, if a citizen contests the scientist's claim, there is a counter-truth claim that the citizen is hoping will be accepted. It is in this sense that speech acts are oriented towards understanding, which presumably will lead to agreement about contested issues and resulting actions. However, the emotions and interests of both parties may prevent any agreement and may even enlarge the conflict.

Fifth, scientific knowledge, while it has a special status in the debate, is not the deciding factor. The findings of science are part of a much larger conversa-tion, where politics, economics, private concerns, beliefs and social relationships all have essential roles to play. The most unfruitful way to think about the climate change debate is as a contest, with the winner being the person who gets the science right. A much more fruitful viewpoint concerns the alignment of societal concerns and actions to make the world a better environ-ment for people.

Sixth, people making arguments extensively use *association* and *dissociation*. Association processes join separate elements so that one is associated with another, positively or negatively. In our family vacation example, one person might say, 'Not that beach! It's just like beach X, with too many people, too many rowdy parties and lots of jellyfish.' Dissociation is the opposite: separation of elements that are commonly thought of together. A vacation example might be, 'We always think that the OK Restaurant will be fun for all, but, really, we haven't had a good time there in the past three years.'

Using association or dissociation also means that the person making the argument selects supporting evidence carefully. The *selection* of the facts of the case is thus supremely important in the efficacy of the argument: choices reveal both what the person thinks will be most convincing and what may be counted on as agreements. Moreover, the *interpretation* of facts is important, especially in distinguishing different arguments that use the same agreed-on facts. In climate change, for instance, many agree that concentrations of greenhouse gases are rising, but there are many interpretations of these data.

A final point (for now) is that agreement – like disagreement – is almost never total. Rather, there are degrees of adherence to arguments and degrees of probability that people assign to them. The goal then is to create more agreement through argument and discussion. In the climate change arena, most of the arguments about taking action concern a future in which the uncertainties are very large – some say they amount to indeterminacy. Therefore, uniform agreement cannot be expected. Indeed, this study is an investigation into partial agreements, based on one or multiple network ties, and how those partial agreements can be built upon.

A Methodology for Comparative Analysis of Arguments

I have used a structured approach to analyse and compare the arguments in 100 documents and public statements explicitly directed to global environmental debates (see Appendix 2 for a list of the documents). I focused principally on documents related to specific proposals for political, economic and social changes to address issues raised in the global climate change debate. I tried to include something from every source I could think of or find (from internet searches, conversations with researchers and activists, and so on). The set of documents includes scientific journal articles and reports, environmental 'activist' statements (environmental social movement groups), cultural/ethnic group statements (for example First Nations in Canada, deep ecologists and ecofeminists), negotiating positions and other policy-oriented statements (from industrialized and developing countries), and media articles or reports. There's even a collection of pictures (Document #77).

The purpose of analysing documents and presentations within the global climate change debate is to discern whether these demonstrate a basis (or several bases) for agreement about policies and other actions to address climate change. By looking at various elements of the documents and presentations,

I should be able to see whether different discourses are cut off from each other, whether they overlap, whether some voices disagree in some (or most) elements but agree in others, and so on. If, for example, certain clusters of elements are tightly correlated with each other and not at all with other clusters, there would be little basis for agreement; people would simply be talking to their in-groups and past other groups, emphasizing their disagreements.

Earlier attempts, including at least one in-depth analysis, have been made to classify the arguments made in the climate change debate. Earlier studies attempted to attribute people's views of nature, the value of the environment and climate change specifically to demographic characteristics – for example, different studies have found weak correlations between age and pro-environmental attitudes (Dunlap, 1991). One theory is that the wisdom that comes with old age and/or the idealism of the young predisposes those groups to an expansive view of global citizenship and caring for the Earth. Other researchers, however, have shown that demographic characteristics are poor predictors of attitudes towards the environment and that cultural beliefs are much more explanatory (Jaeger et al, 1993).

What is meant by 'cultural beliefs'? Here the phrase means people's deep assumptions – often so deeply ingrained that they are unspoken and unrecognized – about how the world is organized and what relationships are 'natural' or 'right' among people in society and between human beings and the rest of Nature. Cultural beliefs are thus equivalent to the category of worldview in the analytic framework I have presented.

Cultural explanations have included several theories. One well-known theory is Maslow's hierarchy of needs, which posits that only when people's primary needs for food and shelter are met will they seek to satisfy more aesthetic and altruistic needs, such as a good environment. This makes intuitive sense; for instance, a person who is hungry is unlikely to care whether or not he or she has high-quality art on the walls. But the theory fails to explain why people starve rather than part with family heirlooms or compromise their religious taboos about food or betray their countries (Douglas et al, 1998).

Cultural anthropologists such as Steve Rayner and Michael Thompson (Thompson et al 1990; Thompson, Rayner et al, 1998), developing Mary Douglas's cultural theory, identify four 'myths of nature' that guide people's arguments about the problem and proposed solutions. Nature can be thought of as *benign* (able to renew itself no matter what human beings do to it), *perverse/tolerant* (robust, but with the possibility that thresholds may be breached and that irrecoverable damage may result), *ephemeral* (delicately balanced, easily capable of collapse), or *capricious* (essentially unknowable and unpredictable). Except for the last (which does not allow for policy to address climate change), Thompson and Rayner associate these myths of nature with institutional voices in the climate change debate:

- Those who think of nature as benign also tend to think of climate change as resulting from a failure to account for the value of natural resources in market transactions; the solution to this problem is to be found within the market, by removing price distortions or privatizing resources or having the government set markets for them.
- Those who think of nature as perverse/tolerant also tend to diagnose the climate change problem as one of exploding population, which perforce places pressure on natural resources; the solution lies in family planning, the availability of technologies that help limit fertility and associated education, especially for women.
- Those who think of nature as ephemeral also tend to argue that the cause of climate change is rampant industrialism and consumerism, which places inordinate demands on natural resources, especially for energy, and allows capitalists to expropriate resources from (for example) farmers; the remedy is to be found in frugality and equality.

So cultural beliefs about nature are relevant, along with people's political interests, economic situation, group and national status, and many other factors. Examining what people have actually said should allow space for other factors and their relative importance.

I limited my analysis to 100 documents published or released between 1992 (the year that the UNFCCC was adopted at the Rio Summit) and 2003 – a good decade after the UNFCCC. Each document has a clear (or clearly implied) policy prescription; in other words, research documents that only report results and perhaps outline further research that is needed were not selected. Discourse on other global environmental issues (for example biodiversity, acid rain, the ozone layer, deforestation and over-fishing) was used as additional evidence and illustration. Documents were publicly available, but I especially sought out documents from the 'grey' literature (newsletters, advocacy briefs and so on); I expected that many or most of the documents from less industrialized countries would be of this type, since the publications in peer-reviewed journals are less common there.

Why did I stop at 100? Many thousands of documents have been written about climate change, and it would be impossible to find and catalogue them all. Instead, I searched and analysed until I was no longer seeing different arguments, just repetitions of previous ones. Of course, I can make no claims about the relative prevalence of any argument.

I reviewed the documents, identified the argument itself and four primary rhetorical dimensions:

1 Who is making the statement and what group or groups are associated with the speaker or writer? How is this person or group influential (positive and negative)?
2 What are the bases of the claim(s) – i.e. what type of evidence is being used?

3   What is the worldview of the speaker or writer, especially as it relates to the viewpoint expressed about the relationship between people and the rest of nature?
4   What are the actions the speaker or writer is proposing?

Since it is probable that secondary and tertiary arguments, lines of evidence and worldviews could provide a basis for agreement, I included them in my document analysis. Similarly, since it is possible for people to agree on specific actions without agreeing on the reasons for those actions, I included any proposed actions in the analysis. As a first step, I filled out the template in Table 4.1 for each document. The next chapter presents the results of this analysis, a clustering of the major arguments.

When I had a table like this filled out for each document (the complete set can be found at www.earthscan.co.uk/dcc), I clustered the arguments themselves into 'families' that were similar in their claims and evidence. This allows a more detailed comparative analysis – the next level of analysis beyond the information in Table 4.1 – for each individual argument. Again, the goal was comparative analysis of arguments to discern bases for potential agreement on actions that could or should be taken to address climate change.

Table 4.1 *Template for first-order document/presentation analysis*

Document Number and Citation
Authority of speaker/writer
Primary:
Secondary:
Tertiary:
Notes
Type of argument
Primary:
Secondary:
Tertiary:
Notes
Type of evidence
Primary:
Secondary:
Tertiary:
Notes:
Worldview/view of nature
Primary:
Secondary:
Tertiary:
Notes:
Action(s) proposed
Primary:
Secondary:
Tertiary:
Notes

One way to cluster the arguments is to determine where they are in terms of the 'stases', a classical tool that provides the following categories (Fahnestock and Secor, 1983):

1   People must agree that something has happened – a matter of fact or conjecture. For the purposes of the study, the question is usually framed as establishing either or both that the concentration of greenhouse gases in the atmosphere has been rising and/or the global mean temperature has risen over the 19th and 20th centuries.

2   People must agree about how to define the fact(s). In practical terms, arguing about definitions can send the argument back to the first stasis. For example, in this case, some people making arguments define the phenomena established in the first stasis as climate change. Others accept the 'facts' of rising concentrations and mean temperature and yet disagree that these facts can be defined as the beginning of long-term climate change.

3   People need to agree about the causes of the phenomena that are the subject of the argument.[2] In the case of climate change, this is often a sticking point. People may agree that atmospheric concentrations and global mean temperature are rising, and that this may be defined as climate change. But can climate change be attributed to human emissions of so-called greenhouse gases?

4   People need to agree about the quality or value of the phenomena. Is it bad or good, serious or trivial? In this stasis, other facts and definitions may be brought in; for example, an argument about treatment with placebos will often involve a definition of the right relationship between doctor and patient. In the case of climate change, the argument at this stage relates to the seriousness of the situation, which may relate to the views of nature discussed above. If a person thinks nature is essentially fragile, he or she will likely believe that human interference in the climate system is a very serious matter indeed.

5   People need to agree that they must take action. In ancient legal use, this stasis was associated with reaching a verdict and passing sentence, but of course action can take many forms. The call to action depends on whether those addressed agree that the seriousness of the situation warrants actions that they can take. In the climate change debate, the calls to action are various and aimed at universal audiences that may be defined differently – for instance, global citizens or Nature lovers.

These frameworks and concepts help to characterize the arguments as arguments and to provide a basis for comparison. For example, a 'deep ecologist' might argue that humanity's true nature has been violated in industrialization, thus associating the true nature of people with a kind of primitive lifestyle. Moreover, the deep ecologist would probably be arguing at the third or fourth stases, since the major points have to do with the cause of the problem (the human embrace of industrialization) and its seriousness (violation of humanity's true nature). In contrast, a scientist might argue that it is human destiny to control nature and reap the benefit of natural resources, thus associating the true nature of people with techno-scientific decision-making. The scientist may be arguing at the fifth stasis, focusing on the ways people can manage nature and industry better. The elements being associated or dissociated within the arguments provide insights into potential bases for agreement among argument-makers. Both can be seen as arguments about definition (of the true nature of human beings) or causes (a relationship gone wrong in the past or simple mistakes that can be corrected in the future), so it is important to examine the evidence for the categories.

I expected that comparing the families of arguments would reveal sets of elements that are closely correlated in each family. For example, a set of correlated elements could consist of the following:

- Noted scientist as the source of the document or presentation;
- Quantitative data as evidence (measurements, equations, etc);
- A worldview that posits human beings as controllers of Nature and Nature as highly resilient to human interference; and
- Proposals to reduce carbon dioxide emissions using a carbon tax.

If all of these elements are strongly associated with each other and not at all with alternative elements, this analysis would indicate that scientific voices in the debate talk to each other but not to non-scientific audiences, despite ubiquitous calls for scientific communication. However, if scientists typically appeal to the authority of the UNFCCC (perhaps as a secondary argument), this gesture to the authority of international law gives them something in common with environmentalist groups, who make the same appeal.

I expected that the most interesting and potentially fruitful correlations would be at the margins of the analysis, for example two secondary types of arguments that are widely shared across the boundaries of science, social solidarity and politics/policy.

But enough of what I expected. The next chapter starts to show what I found.

Notes

1 A premise is a proposition upon which an argument is based; a warrant is the way a debater connects evidence to a premise; metaphor is a way of connecting one thing to another by pointing out their similarities; and an enthymeme is an abbreviated formulation of an argument in which the conclusion or premises are left unexpressed.
2 This is a stasis inserted by Jeanne Fahnestock and Marie Secor to account for the contemporary emphasis on causal inquiry in the social, political and natural sciences.

References

Austin, J. L. (1962) *How To Do Things with Words*, Harvard University Press, Cambridge, MA

Bitzer, L. (1968) 'The rhetorical situation', *Philosophy and Rhetoric*, vol 1

Burke, K. (1989) *On Symbols and Society*, University of Chicago Press, Chicago, IL

Douglas, M. (1982) 'Cultural bias', in M. Douglas (ed) *In the Active Voice*, Routledge, London

Douglas, M., Gasper, D., Ney, S. and Thompson, M. (1998) 'Human needs and wants', in S. Rayner and E. L. Malone (eds) *Human Choice and Climate Change, Volume 1: The Societal Framework*, Battelle Press, Columbus, OH

Dunlap, R. E. (1991) 'Trends in public opinion toward environmental issues: 1965–1990', *Society and Natural Resources*, vol 4, pp285–312

Fahnestock, J. and Secor, M. (1983) 'Teaching argument: A theory of types', *College Composition and Communication*, vol 34, pp20–30

Habermas, J. (1984) *The Theory of Communicative Action: Reason and the Rationalization of Society*, vol 1, trans. T. McCarthy, Beacon Press, Cambridge, MA

Habermas, J. (1987) *The Theory of Communicative Action: Lifeworld and System: A Critique of Functionalist Reason*, vol 2, trans. T. McCarthy, Polity Press, Cambridge, UK

Habermas, J. (1989) *Structural Transformation of the Public Sphere: An Inquiry into a Category of Bourgeois Society*, Polity Press, Cambridge, UK

Jaeger, C., Dürrenberger, G., Kastenholz, H. and Truffer, B. (1993) 'Determinants of environmental action with regard to climate change', *Climatic Change*, vol 23, pp193–211

Klumpp, J. F. (1993) 'A rapprochement between dramatism and argument', *Argumentation and Advocacy*, vol 29, pp148–163

Ling, D. (1989) 'A pentadic analysis of Senator Edward Kennedy's address to the people of Massachusetts, 25 July 1969', in S. K. Foss (ed) *Rhetorical Criticism: Exploration and Practice*, Prospect Heights, IL

Perelmen, C. and Olbrechts-Tyteca, L. (1969) *The New Rhetoric: A Treatise on Argumentation*, trans. J. Wilkinson and P. Weaver, 1971 reprint, University of Notre Dame Press, Notre Dame, IN

Thompson, M., Ellis, R. and Wildavsky, A. (1990) *Cultural Theory*, Westview, Boulder, CO

Thompson, M., Rayner, S. et al (1998) 'Cultural discourses', in S. Rayner and E. L. Malone (eds) *Human Choice and Climate Change, Volume 2: The Societal Framework*, Battelle Press, Columbus, OH

Toulmin, S. (1958) *The Uses of Argument*, Cambridge University Press, Cambridge, UK

Wells, S. (1996) *Sweet Reason: Rhetoric and the Discourses of Modernity*, University of Chicago Press, Chicago, IL

Vatz, R. E. (1973) 'The myth of the rhetorical situation', *Philosophy and Rhetoric*, vol 6, p154

5

Finding Common Ground:
The Features of the Arguments

I grouped the 100 documents described in the previous chapter into 'families of arguments'. There are at least 11 coherent arguments about the hypothesis that human activities contribute to climate change, the degree of threat that results from possible climate change, the basis for acting in response to the threat and the specific actions that are necessary. I have termed these families of arguments 'No Problem!', 'Climate Change Could Be Good for You', 'Science Provides Knowledge about Climate Change', 'More Modernization Is the Cure' (six different families – 'Focus on the Political Process', 'Reform the Energy System', 'Mitigate Climate Change', 'Prepare to Adapt', 'Get the Prices Right' and 'Mitigate and Adapt'), 'Inequality Is the Problem', and 'Rift with Nature'.

Table 5.1 shows how many members of each family there are within the 100 documents, as well as a brief overview of the analysis using the three rhetorical tools (the stases, association/dissociation and definition/cause and effect) discussed in Chapter 4. Note that the 'shares' of arguments in this set of documents can not be taken to represent the importance or even the proportional presence of different arguments in the actual debate; for instance, no one could claim that 'No Problem!' arguments constitute three per cent of all arguments made.

Next I briefly discuss each family and analyse example arguments. Grouping into families and characterizing the families rhetorically helps to map the debate space. For each family, the discussion includes an example and, in most cases, the analysis table for the example.

Family #1: No Problem!

One family of arguments does not feel a sense of urgency about climate change because the family members deny that climate change is a reality. Many of these family members claim that climate change is an easily falsified hypothesis. Or they claim that climate change is possible but the science is very

Table 5.1 *Overview of document set and rhetorical classifications*

	Number of arguments	Stasis	Associate climate change with...	Argument from...
No Problem!	3	1	Bad science	Definition
Climate Change Could Be Good for You	8	2 and 4	Normal problems that human beings have shown they can solve	Definition
Science Provides Knowledge about Climate Change	9	3	An issue open to scientific inquiry	Definition
More Modernization Is the Cure (six families)	48	5	One more problem that can be addressed through politics, economics and technology	Definition, cause and effect
Inequality Is the Problem	17	3 and 4	Inequality of nations and people	Definition, cause and effect
Rift with Nature	15	3 and 4	Unhealthy, subject–object relationship with nature	Definition, cause and effect

Note: See www.earthscan.co.uk/dcc for a first-stage analysis of each of the 100 arguments.

uncertain. Or the claim is that climate change may be happening, but the causes are unrelated to any human activities. Their arguments are located at the first stasis, and they hold that nothing we can call human-induced climate change has been demonstrated. Of the 100 documents, 3 are clearly in this family.

Scientists or analysts in this family express scepticism that climate change is a plausible scientific argument – or, if they allow that climate change is possible, they dispute its anthropogenic causes. Thus, they argue, people need not be concerned about reducing emissions of greenhouse gases. These family members claim that the scientific evidence can be countered by other scientific evidence; for example, the historical record may be said to demonstrate that carbon dioxide concentrations fluctuate without correlation to temperature, so the correlation of the past two centuries does not indicate a causal relationship. Or cosmic rays cause climate warming, not greenhouse gases. Or the climate models are too crude for us to place any faith in their projections/predictions. Or scientists are simply engaging in what one US Senator called 'junk science' and only concerned to keep the research dollars coming by continuing to investigate the 'threat' of climate change.

The science itself may not be contested, but the degree of uncertainty, say some, is such that we are unjustified in taking any mitigating actions – especially if these actions are costly.

A representative example of the scientifically based 'No Problem!' argument is the paper by Richard Lindzen (no date), a professor at Massachusetts Institute of Technology (see Table 5.2). Lindzen rhetorically associates himself with the debate within the scientific community and dissociates the scientific debate from the political activities that brought climate

Table 5.2 *First-step analysis of Lindzen argument*

#46:	Lindzen, Richard S. (n.d.) 'Global warming: The origin and nature of the alleged scientific consensus', Cato Institute, Washington, DC, downloaded March 2003

Authority of speaker/writer

Primary:	Lindzen is a prominent sceptic, well respected as a scientist (Massachusetts Institute of Technology) but also affiliated with Cato, which is seen as ideological.

Type of argument

Primary:	'As a scientist, I can find no substantive basis for the warming scenarios being popularly described.'
Secondary:	'Moreover, according to many studies I have read by economists, agronomists and hydrologists, there would be little difficulty adapting to such warming if it were to occur.'
Tertiary:	'Present hysteria formally began in the summer of 1988', with a hot summer and James Hansen's meaningless statement, and quickly became a 'global warming circus'; scientific debate OK, politicization dreadful; warming does fit with other agendas, such as energy efficiency, reduced oil from the Middle East, dissatisfaction with industrialization, international competition, enhanced revenue from carbon taxes and enhanced power.

Type of evidence

Primary:	'Such was also the conclusion of the recent National Research Council report of adapting to global change. Many aspects of the catastrophic scenario have already been largely discounted by the scientific community.'
Secondary:	Examines the arguments; agrees that CO_2 in the atmosphere has been increasing, but says an inaccurate model was used to predict a doubling of pre-industrial levels by 2030 – 'The simple picture of the greenhouse mechanism is seriously oversimplified.' – water vapour and clouds account for most of the effect, convection must be taken into account, models cannot duplicate the motions of the atmosphere, feedbacks are highly uncertain and not understood – predictions are exaggerated.
Tertiary:	History of the political process; Al Gore, environmental advocacy groups, Claudine Schneider ('scientists may disagree, but we can hear Mother Earth, and she is crying'), refusal of *Science* to print Lindzen's critique, various actors, Michael Openheimer/EDF, Greenpeace, etc.
Notes:	Puts 'greenhouse theory' in quotes, refers to 'popular presentation' and 'crude idea' of this theory.

Worldview/view of nature

Primary:	'Improved technology and increased societal wealth are what allow society to deal with environmental threats most effectively.'

Action(s) proposed

Primary:	Allow science to take its course, admitting the flaws of the models – get politics out of the picture.
Secondary:	Focus on the control of societal instability.

Note: See www.earthscan.co.uk/dcc for a first-stage analysis of each of the 100 arguments.

change to the attention of governments. He stakes out his ground by saying, 'as a scientist, I can find no substantive basis for the warming scenarios being popularly described'. On the dissociative side, he characterizes the politics as 'a global warming circus' based on a 'crude idea' (not even a theory) that fits in with other political agendas, such as the push to reduce oil imports from the Middle East. This is an argument from definition: climate change is a scientific problem, not a political one.

His conclusion: climate change does not exist as a scientific phenomenon.

Family #2: Climate Change May Be Good for You

Members of this family claim that climate change (if it happens) may be 'good for you', and in any case would be so slow that people could adapt. In all of these cases, the proposal is the same: do nothing. There is nothing to worry about because matters will take care of themselves and will probably entail more positive than negative changes. This family of arguments is located at the second stasis; most acknowledge that long-term changes in the climate are apparent; however, they argue that these changes should not be defined as a 'problem' to be addressed. Or the argument may be at the fourth stasis, accepting the evidence of climate change and even of human causes – but, still, they say, the situation is not a problem. Climate change may be good for people. Of the 100 documents, 8 are in this family.

Many of the argument-makers who deny exigence express faith that people will be able to adjust as manifestations of climate change become apparent. Therefore, they argue, it is unwise to take speculative and (probably) expensive actions now, when we really don't know, first, if climate change will occur; second, what the impacts will be; and third, what climate change will mean for each region and locality.

A representative example of this argument is the article by Jesse Ausubel (see Table 5.3), in which he provides a long list of beneficial adaptations that people have made to climate. Ausubel's argument is an associative one – adapting to a changing climate is an old problem, with a long history of successful adaptations. In contrast to analysts who carefully document the uniqueness of the current climate change problem (the anthropogenic causes, the likely magnitude, the long timescale), Ausubel attempts to 'normalize' the problem by briefly describing past adaptations and then listing a long catalogue of ways we have come to adapt to our current climate in ingenious ways: cisterns and dams, tractors, new crop cultivars, information technologies, tide tables, irrigation scheduling, weather forecasts, agricultural credit banks, national parks, green political parties, flood insurance, food preservatives, light bulbs and refrigeration/air-conditioning. In fact, we have adapted so well that our industries, transportation and daily lives are becoming more and more impervious to climate considerations. Surely we can extend our ingenuity to adapt as changes happen.

Again, this is an argument from definition: climate change is a familiar and age-old problem and, because we have seen it before, we have many ways to deal with it. Ausubel is at the fourth stasis here. He accepts the evidence and the definition of the evidence as at least the possibility of climate change. He ignores the third stasis by not engaging with the issue of whether or not human beings have caused climate change. At the fourth stasis, his argument is that climate change is not a 'problem' at all, much less a serious problem calling for action.

Table 5.3 *First-step analysis of Ausubel argument*

#3:	Ausubel, Jesse H. (2001) 'Some ways to lessen worries about climate', The Electricity Journal, January/February, pp24–33
Authority of speaker/writer	
Primary:	Ausubel is 'Director of the Program for the Human Environment at The Rockefeller University, New York. He was one of the main organizers of the first United Nations World Climate Conference, held in Geneva in 1979.'
Notes:	'This article is adapted from the keynote address to the Business Roundtable's National Summit on Technology and Climate Change', 31 August 2000.
Type of argument	
Primary:	It is likely that human emissions of GHGs will change the climate but we do not know how and probably cannot know. 'But gambling with the climate does not strike me as a good bet.'
Secondary:	'Societies are always trying to climate-proof themselves' (p25) and many successful adaptations exist.
Tertiary:	Technological change is a continuing process that demonstrates our adaptability, our potential to design offsets and engage in prevention strategies such as the Zero-Emission Power Plant (ZEPP).
Type of evidence	
Primary:	Graphics showing technological cycles and improvements (recording media, RAM, transportation modes and power plant size), with accompanying text.
Secondary:	Long lists of ways we adapt to climate, e.g. 'from antifreeze, air-conditioning and corn futures markets to windshield wipers, radar and domed stadiums' (p25).
Worldview/view of nature	
Primary:	Nature is essentially unpredictable; people can control their behaviour.
Action(s) proposed	
Primary:	'So, I say, let us prepare, just in case. Purchase some insurance. … Public and private entities should research and invest in all three' forms of climate insurance: adaptation, offsets and prevention (p25).
Secondary:	'We should choose long-term solutions for emissions compatible with the evolution of the energy system. This means shift to methane, focus offsets on the carbon in methane, prepare the hydrogen economy and anticipate the nuclear millennium that will follow our Methane Age' (p33).

Note: See www.earthscan.co.uk/dcc for a first-stage analysis of each of the 100 arguments.

Family #3: Science Provides Knowledge about Climate Change

This family of explicitly scientific arguments typically takes climate change as a starting datum, which the audience will agree is a fact. The questions to be investigated within this basic agreement concern the degree of change and its possible impacts. Nine of the documents examined are in this family; however, my requirement that documents propose one or more actions eliminated many dozens of documents, because many scientific studies stop short of making explicit policy recommendations. Most come to the familiar conclusion that 'more research is needed'. For example, scientists who perform core sampling to reconstruct past concentrations of greenhouse gases or who describe the atmospheric chemistry of greenhouse gas decay in the atmosphere leave it to others to use their findings in a constructed, policy-relevant argument.

Because not even all scientists can be counted upon to take the same view of climate change, scientific writers provide sometimes lengthy introductions to their journal articles, framing the climate change issue as one of both science (with citations) and policy (with reference to the UNFCCC). These introductions legitimate the scientific inquiry that is being reported; they define, in part, the scope of the investigation (for example some aspect of climate change). In such scientific arguments, the potential for climate change is an assumption, not a term of the argument. Researchers then define the issues and questions relevant to the research they are reporting. Next come the description of the methodology (including, typically, a computer-based model), results and findings. The final section suggests policy implications and further research.

So far I have described an example of the standard genre of scientific articles. Although the structure and style of the scientific article is one source of its authority, with the identity of the author(s) and the reputation of the journal adding to that authority, the content of the argument itself and the evidence should carry the bulk of the responsibility for convincing the audience, since science is based on evidence.

A representative example of this argument is an article by scientists from the Economic Research Service of the US Department of Agriculture (see Table 5.4). These researchers are 'ecological economists' who used a computer-based model (the Future Agricultural Resources Model, FARM) to make projections of changes in land use and land cover using different scenarios of climate and social change. Computer-based modelling is a mainstream method for science-based projections of climate, socio-economic conditions, energy use, greenhouse gas emissions and so on. A large proportion of the article (12 of 24 pages) is spent explaining the architecture of the model, its data sources (three tables and a map) and the modelled relationships.

The authors chose to model land use and land cover (in other words how people are using the land and what vegetation is on it) because these constitute an 'integrating concept' which brings together the productivity of the land, the principal source for human food and fibre, and competition among human beings and other species for food. Thus the scientists intend that an examination of land use and land cover will yield results worth knowing about how both human economy and ecology will respond to climate change. However, the results of the modelled scenarios are ambivalent – 'whether the correlation with a particular economic variable [and forest depletion in Southeast Asia] is positive or negative depends on the global change scenario', they say. The best they can do for a recommendation is to say that climate change (along with population growth and deregulation of agricultural trade) will probably have 'adverse effects on the health and integrity of tropical forest ecosystems', but that improvements in models are needed before scientists can make definitive statements.

This argument contains several notable elements. First, the ethos is unmistakably scientific; typically, the venue is a specialized and technical journal, and there are multiple authors, all from a research organization in a government agency. Thus they associate climate change with other scientific problems: it is open to empirical examination, mathematical manipulation and hypothesis

Table **5.4** *First-step analysis of Darwin et al argument*

#19:	Darwin, Roy, Marinow Tsigas, Jan Lewandrowski and Anton Raneses (1996), 'Land use and cover in ecological economics', Ecological Economics, vol 17, pp157–181
Authority of speaker/writer	
Primary:	The authors were at the Economic Research Service, US Dept of Agriculture.
Type of argument	
Primary:	Land use/cover is an 'integrating concept': (1) 'the main resource governing primary productivity can be defined in terms of land' (p157); (2) 'land remains the primary source of the energy and mass that compose our food and fibre' (p158); (3) 'the most important interaction between human beings and other biological communities is the competition for land' (p158).
Notes:	'A basic premise of ecological economics is that the world economy is embedded in and dependent upon Earth's ecosystem. This dependency is captured by the concept of "throughput" (Boulding, 1966) or "entropic flow" (Georgescu-Roegen, 1971) – the one-way flow of energy and mass through an economy that begins with resources and ends with waste.' (p157)
Type of evidence	
Primary:	'We present a model that integrates economic-ecological activities with land use and cover' (p157); the Future Agricultural Resources Model (FARM), developed at USDA 'to evaluate impacts of global climate change on the world's agricultural system' (p158), which includes a geographical information system (GIS) and a computable general equilibrium (CGE) economic model (description pp159–171).
Notes:	Full-page flowchart of the model, 3 tables and a map re land class endowments.
Worldview/view of nature	
Primary:	'Interactions between economic and ecological phenomena are complex' (p180); 'Whether the correlation with a particular economic variable [and forest depletion in Southeast Asia] is positive or negative depends on the global change scenario.' (p180)
Action(s) proposed	
Primary:	'Results from our scenarios [of global climate change, population growth and deregulation of agricultural trade] indicate that such changes are likely to have adverse effects on the health and integrity of tropical forest ecosystems.' (p180)
Secondary:	'Improved throughput analyses require better tracking of resource stocks (soil, water, forests, fossil fuels, etc.) coupled with waste emission coefficients for various economic sectors. Methods for simulating inter- and intraregional labour migration, investment in human and physical capital, and technological change are needed to conduct dynamic analyses.' (p180)

Note: See www.earthscan.co.uk/dcc for a first-stage analysis of each of the 100 arguments.

testing. They assert that 'interactions between economic and ecological phenomena are complex' but treat these interactions as knowable, and more knowable as models of them are developed. Second, the authors analytically distinguish between climate change and socio-economic conditions. In their model, the two are dissociated, presumably so that the independent effect of climate change can be studied. The effect of this strategy, however, is that the alleged human causes of climate change disappear into the background. Thus this framing of the issue as a scientific problem dissociated from social causes and uncertain social effects is quite different from the close association of climate change and social dimensions that is found in other arguments.

The argument is principally an argument from definition (climate change is a scientific problem), but cause and effect are explored by means of the FARM model. If climate changes like this and socio-economic conditions change like that, then the impacts will be harmful (or benign). This very carefully hedged type of cause-and-effect argument is very typical of scientific studies of climate change – and the type of argument that leaves ample ambiguous space for political proposals. This argument is situated at the third stasis; the scientist-authors are inquiring into how climate change (as a cause) will affect land use and land cover (as results).

Families #4–9: More Modernization Is the Cure

By far the largest number of arguments have in common the underlying assumption that climate change is a serious, possibly catastrophic problem that is at least partially caused by human beings and one that human beings can mitigate with the strategies of modernity: technological change, economic accounting and rational negotiations. These argument-makers have moved to the final stasis – the call to action – indicating agreement on all the previous stases, in other words that something has happened, that 'something' is climate change, it is caused by human activities, and it is a serious problem. Considered as one family, this group is the largest, with 48 of 100 texts in this category. However, the group can be further disaggregated by the foci of their arguments. Families #4–9 share their underlying assumptions about the need for and efficacy of human managerial actions, but they differ in their arguments about where and in what ways the actions should be undertaken.

Agreement along all the stases should indicate a fairly high level of agreement overall, but this is not necessarily the case. I will analyse several examples of different approaches to and proposals for action. Among scientists the different approaches are recognizably disciplinary; that is, political scientists focus on the roles of international agreements and domestic policies, economists focus on the role of markets in preserving natural resources and preventing pollution, and engineers focus on the role of technological change. Among policymakers and environmentally concerned advocates, these lines become blurred; mixed solutions, involving a range of actions from lifestyle changes to renewable energy development to environmental cleanup, come as a palette of recommendations.

One group treats the political process as the essential element of action on climate change; this is Family #4 ('Focus on the Political Process', with 8 members). This family advocates the development and implementation of effective treaties, conventions, protocols and other policy mechanisms. Many political analysts, such as Richard Benedick, cite the Montreal Protocol, under which ozone-depleting substances were phased out and which has been widely regarded as a successful international agreement.

A good example of a more-modernization argument that focuses on political processes is a Worldwatch press release called 'Global war on global warming heats up' (see Table 5.5), a review of *Reading the Weathervane: Climate Policy from Rio to Johannesburg*. The document asserts that in the decade after the UNFCCC was adopted, 'the scientific case for action contin-

Table 5.5 *First-step analysis of Worldwatch argument*

#97:	Worldwatch Institute (2002) 'Global war on global warming heats up', press release, www.worldwatch.org/press/news/2002/08/01

Authority of speaker/writer

Primary:	Worldwatch Institute is a well-known environmentalist group that produces an annual *State of the World* report. In the press release, it describes itself as 'a Washington, DC-based research organization'.
Notes:	This is a review of *Reading the Weathervane: Climate Policy from Rio to Johannesburg* by Seth Dunn.

Type of argument

Primary:	'The scientific case for action continued to strengthen [in 1990–2001, but most policies] have been too weak, only partially implemented or discontinued'; governments have 'failed to develop "diversified portfolios" of policies'; and 'the existence of "perverse practices" – including subsidies for fossil fuel production and consumption … has been a major impediment to climate policymaking.' Emissions have generally risen since 1990 (e.g. in the EU, Japan, US, Australia and Canada), except in Germany (–17.1%), the UK (–4.1%) and Russia (–30.5%). Secondary: India, China and Brazil are not 'rogue emitters' but have been slowing emissions growth, China because of lower coal use and energy efficiency. Tertiary: Lowering emissions will not be costly, as conventional model results indicate.

Type of evidence

Primary:	Stats about emissions, energy intensity, etc.
Secondary:	History of the UNFCCC and international actions based on it.

Worldview/view of nature

Primary:	Human beings have an obligation to reduce GHG emissions.

Action(s) proposed

Primary:	Bring the Kyoto Protocol into force.
Secondary:	Leave the era of voluntary commitments behind.
Tertiary:	Deal with the transportation sector.

Note: See www.earthscan.co.uk/dcc for a first-stage analysis of each of the 100 arguments.

ued to strengthen', but most policies 'have been too weak, only partially implemented or discontinued' and 'the existence of "perverse practices" – including subsidies for fossil fuel production and consumption … has been a major impediment to climate policymaking'. Here the blame for the failure to reduce emissions is laid squarely on the failure of governments to make and implement effective policies – not, for example, on population growth or excessive consumption. The actions proposed are similarly political: bring the Kyoto Protocol into force, forget about 'voluntary' commitments (they don't work) and focus on reducing emissions in the transportation sector.

Worldwatch thus also makes one argument from definition: climate change is a political problem, solvable by political means. The press release also argues that the causes of climate change also can be found in governance, for example 'perverse practices' like subsidies that encourage continued fossil fuel use.

Other argument-makers – here gathered in Family #5 ('Reform the Energy System', 10 members) – focus on the reform of the energy system as the key to forestalling climate change. The technology-focused arguments can be gathered under the term 'ecological modernization'. This is the idea that human beings have the ingenuity to alter their own technologies so they will be environmentally harmless. For example, renewable forms of energy – solar, wind, geothermal and hydro power – can be developed that will meet people's needs without causing environmental damage. This argument is often coupled with arguments for sustainable development, defined as meeting the needs of people without harming the future environment (WCED, 1987).

A good example of a more-modernization argument that focuses on technological change in the energy system is the speech in which John Browne, the CEO of British Petroleum (BP) (or, as the corporation now styles itself, 'Beyond Petroleum'), announced that his corporation had decided to take climate change seriously and initiate some planning and mitigation actions (see Table 5.6). Industrial firms, especially in the energy industry, generally have been opponents of taking action to reduce greenhouse gas emissions, since they often see such actions – developing new technologies, perhaps retiring capital stock before the end of its useful life and perhaps bearing the costs of carbon taxes – as costly for them.

But Browne and BP 'broke ranks' with the rest of the energy industry. His argument associates BP and its employees with the rest of society: 'The passing of some of the old divisions reminds us we are all citizens of one world, and we must take shared responsibility for its future, and for its sustainable development.' Browne says that people who work at BP have these convictions, as do consumers. He uses the metaphor of a journey, with the need for partnerships and accommodations to the interests of all who are on the journey.

Browne then catalogues the actions BP has taken and intends to take. The multinational corporation has reduced oil discharges to the North Sea, invested $100 million to eliminate volatile organic compounds, reduced flaring at its operations in Norway, become a partner in a project to conserve 1.5 million hectares of forests in Bolivia and invested in solar power. He announces BP's plan to have an in-house emissions trading system to reduce emissions and fund research. In the long term, BP will work towards sustainability, 'simultaneously being profitable and responding to the reality and the concerns of the world in which [they] operate'. In other words, industry can change; modernization can combat climate change. Climate change is a technical problem that, like other problems we encounter along life's journey, can be faced and solved. Stated thus, this definition of climate change as a problem is fairly close to the definition of climate change as a scientific problem. In both cases, the problem can be investigated and solutions can be found. (In his optimism, Browne is like Ausubel, described in Family 2; unlike Ausubel, though, Browne is rolling up his sleeves and getting to work on a list of specific actions – and he doesn't think climate change will be good for humanity.)

Broadening from concerns about the energy system to consider all forms of mitigation (reductions of greenhouse gas emissions and development of carbon sinks, for example by planting trees) are the arguments that constitute Family #6 ('Mitigate Climate Change', 10 members). Climate mitigation arguments posit emissions reductions as the way to 'solve' the climate problem, whether those reductions come from reforming the energy system,

Table 5.6 *First-step analysis of Browne argument*

#47:	Browne, John (1997) climate change speech given at Stanford University, available at http://icc370.igc.org/bp.htm
Authority of speaker/writer	
Primary:	Browne at the time (and until 2007) was CEO of BP, one of the world's largest petroleum companies.
Type of argument	
Primary:	'The passing of some of the old divisions reminds us we are all citizens of one world, and we must take shared responsibility for its future, and for its sustainable development.' People who work at BP have these convictions, so do consumers.
Secondary:	'The time to consider the policy dimensions of climate change is not when the link between greenhouse gases and climate change is conclusively proven – but when the possibility cannot be discounted and is taken seriously by the society of which we are part. We in BP have reached that point.'
Type of evidence	
Primary:	The science is uncertain, but scientists and others take the possibility seriously (i.e. we are all in this together); metaphor of a journey, with partnerships and accommodations to the interests of all who are on the journey.
Secondary:	Factual evidence – CO_2 like a small weight that overbalances, and only a small fraction comes from transport, and only a fraction of that from BP (~95 Mt).
Tertiary:	Catalogue of actions that show BP is proactive: reduced oil discharges to the North Sea, investing $100m to eliminate volatile organic compounds (VOCs), reduced flaring in Norway; example of project in Bolivia to conserve 1.5m ha of forests; example of investment in solar energy.
Worldview/view of nature	
We can correct our mistakes through more management and technology.	
Action(s) proposed	
Primary:	First, do the low-hanging fruit: control own emissions, fund research, initiatives for joint implementation (JI), develop alternative fuels, contribute to public policy debate.
Secondary:	Strive towards sustainability, 'simultaneously being profitable and responding to the reality and the concerns of the world in which you operate'.

Note: See www.earthscan.co.uk/dcc for a first-stage analysis of each of the 100 arguments.

changing industrial processes such as aluminium smelting and cement manufacture, controlling methane emissions from agricultural operations and landfills, creating carbon sinks through forest growth and management, or other proposed controls.

However, the argument-makers in Family #7 ('Prepare to Adapt', 4 members) argue that countries, businesses and individuals must plan adaptation strategies for changes in the climate that are underway and 'in the pipeline' from current and projected emissions. For example, if a likely impact of climate change is a different precipitation pattern, then farmers and policymakers ought to be planning for alternative crops, varieties and management strategies. Between its Second Assessment in 1996 and the Third Assessment in 2001, the Intergovernmental Panel on Climate Change expanded the focus of its impacts working group to include adaptation, vulnerability and sustainable development (see Document #48). The Fourth Assessment continues and amplifies this emphasis.

Family #8 ('Get the Prices Right', 5 members) comprises economists and others who argue that there are economically viable and efficient ways to reduce emissions and take other actions to address climate change. Ecological economists may hold this view and couple it with arguments promoting the concept of sustainable development. It was a mistake to treat natural resources as free goods, as is done in classical economics, they say; but once we can figure out good ways to price water, parkland, biodiversity and other natural goods, the market will (help) take care of the environment.

A good example of a more-modernization argument from an economic perspective is a report by Jae Edmonds and Michael J. Scott, *International Emissions Trading and Global Climate Change* (see Table 5.7). This report was commissioned and issued by the Pew Center on Global Climate Change, which aims to provide scientifically based information about climate change to an informed but non-scientific audience. Edmonds and Scott examine the question of how costly it would be to reduce emissions enough to stabilize the climate. They take a century-scale view, reasoning that the total amount of greenhouse gases emitted matters, but *when* they are emitted matters less. Similarly, reductions should be taken *where* it is least expensive to do so – usually in countries with little capital stock (such as coal-fired industrial plants) that might become useless (if emissions were prohibited).

Emissions trading, they argue (in other words allowing some countries to 'buy' emissions reductions elsewhere instead of reducing domestic emissions), should reduce the cost of a climate mitigation programme (although Edmonds and Scott point out that actual savings depend on the design of the programme). Thus their recommendations are to allow emissions trading in any scheme to reduce emissions worldwide and to ensure that the programme is designed to maximize savings.

This argument defines climate change narrowly as a problem of cost calculation. It is an argument that assumes that its readers agree that climate change is a problem and a human-caused problem. It therefore focuses on determining a least-cost pathway to mitigation. And, although this is strictly an economic analysis, many of the climate change arguments take as at least their ostensible subject whether or not it is too costly for the world to deal with a problem that is so uncertain and so far off.

This report's contribution to that sub-debate is to show both that costs can be reduced and that the overall cost of mitigation is very small relative to the likely economic product of the world over the 21st century.

In Family #9 ('Mitigate and Adapt', 10 members) are debaters who call for broad-based actions, both mitigation and adaptation. This family makes little or no distinction among mitigation and adaptation activities but only seeks to propose doable actions that often provide 'co-benefits' in, for example, smog reduction, traffic congestion and water availability. The California National Assessment Report (Document #17), for instance, proposes an emphasis on 'multiple benefits' and 'no regrets' strategies (the latter being actions that cost less than the savings that would result), such as energy efficiency, waste reduction, better cost signals to consumers about the use of resources, floodplain management, public education, limits on the footprint of development,

Table 5.7 *First-step analysis of Edmonds and Scott argument*

#15:	Edmonds, Jae, Michael J. Scott et al (1999) *International Emissions Trading and Global Climate Change*, Pew Center on Global Climate Change, Washington, DC

Authority of speaker/writer
Primary: Jae Edmonds was one of the first modellers of emissions and energy related to global climate change and an early integrated assessment modeller.
Secondary: The Pew Center is an advocacy group but strives for balance in its reports.

Type of argument
Primary: Because emissions mitigation addresses a century-scale problem, costs must be low if action is to be undertaken (i.e. there is no immediate benefit resulting from costs).
Secondary: Theory favours trading to lower costs, but actual costs depend on the design of the programme.

Type of evidence
Primary: Discussion of the principles of trade.
Secondary: Model results showing benefits of emissions trading relative to no trading.

Worldview/view of nature
Primary: Human beings and human activities are the focus; nature is secondary.

Action(s) proposed
Primary: Allow emissions trading in any scheme to reduce emissions.
Secondary: 'Programmes must be carefully designed to assure that the potential gains from trade are realized' (page iv). Actual costs likely to be lower because 'models do not include the various measurement, verification, trading and enforcement costs that would characterize any real trading system' (page iv).

Note: See www.earthscan.co.uk/dcc for a first-stage analysis of each of the 100 arguments.

management of stormwater runoff to let water percolate into the soil, careful coastal land use planning and so on.

Theoretically, it is too facile to simply fuse Families #4–9 into a single family of arguments that share the conviction that thoroughly modern people can fix their thoroughly modern problems. Hence, I have grouped the families that share this conviction but separated them into families, recognizing their real, and sometimes vehement, disagreements with each other. For example, the Worldwatch assertion that voluntary commitments do not work is a realization that most corporations will not undertake emissions-reducing activities unless required to do so (in contrast to Browne's argument about BP). Edmonds and Scott also recognize that there is no cost incentive for corporations or governments to address climate change. However, Browne, using inclusive pronouns, asserts that corporations, after all, are made up of people; and that these people-run corporations will realize that it is in their own interests to undertake emissions-reducing activities.

This brief description of some of the arguments made at the last stasis – the call to action – shows that the common agreement among argument-makers that *something* can be done may be undermined or even negated by disagreements about *what* should be done.

Family #10: Inequality Is the Problem

Another family of arguments constructs climate change as one in a long list of manifestations of the inequality of countries and people – the rich and powerful versus the poor and powerless. Over the course of centuries, a world system of nations has evolved that has preserved and increased inequality through various types of colonialization. In Immanuel Wallerstein's (1974 and 1983) terms, the core countries retain power over countries on the periphery through terms of trade, control of technology and so on. Within the climate change debate, this is typically thought of as the argument of the so-called South or the developing countries. Of the 100 texts, 17 are members of this family. Perhaps a bit surprisingly, the authorship of the documents is split about equally between Southern and Northern authors. These arguments move back to the middle stases, being concerned with the root cause of climate change (third stasis) and the meaning or value of the issue (fourth stasis).

An example of this argument is a text from the Indian Centre for Science and the Environment (see Table 5.8). The authors, Anil Agarwal and Sunita Narain (1996), argue that rich countries are attempting to associate the political processes surrounding global warming with other political processes. Global warming, they say, is just one more issue on the agenda of rich countries who wish to preserve the present inequality. A pattern has been set up: an issue of supposedly common concern arises, and rich counties, whose colonialism/imperialism has caused the problem, impose the 'solution' on poor nations, at the cost of the latter. Ahmed and Ahmed (Document #11) put this point more strongly, calling the actions of rich countries 'the assault on nature', which is now being mimicked by the developing countries.

In this case, proposals espoused by rich countries, under the UNFCCC, provide for emissions to be reduced based on a fraction of annual emissions. That is, the present status quo, the current levels of emissions, would be accepted as the starting basis for any mitigation action. Agarwal and Narain, speaking from the perspective of a developing country, argue that the two – the present unequal status of countries and global warming – should be dissociated, and that global warming instead should be treated as a pollution problem (in other words associated with other pollution regimes, rather than with the unequal world system); the principal polluters would then be responsible for reducing pollution and paying for the damage. In this case, total emissions from the start of the Industrial Revolution would be considered and counted against the principal emitters; the starting point for any future mitigation would be emissions per capita (in other words industrialized countries would be responsible for much greater mitigation than non-industrialized countries).

The demographer Anthony J. McMichael's argument (Document #66) rests on his identification of 'the one underlying problem [which] is the entrenched inequality between rich and poor countries', manifested in '(1) rapid, poverty-related, population growth and land degradation in poor

Table 5.8 *First-step analysis of Agarwal and Narain argument*

#1:	Agarwal, Anil and Sunita Narain (1996), 'The atmospheric rights of all people on Earth: Why is it necessary to move towards the "ultimate objective" of the Framework Convention on Climate Change?', Centre for Science and the Environment, www.cseindia.org/html/cmp/cmp31.htm

Authority of speaker/writer

Primary:	Agarwal and Narain are known for definitive statements of the developing country perspective on climate change (cf. *Global Warming in an Unequal World*).
Secondary:	The authority of the CSE as a voice in the climate change issue, beginning before the UNFCCC and continuing by NGO participation in further COPs.

Type of argument

Primary:	The world is unequal; rich countries have caused global warming ('historical emissions') and should pay the true costs of their consumption ('polluter pays') and should set up time-bound targets for greenhouse gas emissions reduction.

Type of evidence

Primary:	Historical recounting of events in negotiations: first, ozone, which 'remains a weak treaty', then the Agarwal and Narain rebuttal of the World Resources Institute position, and their continuing role in climate issues.
Secondary:	Facts about total emissions vs. per capita emissions.
Notes:	The form of the argument is 'What the developed countries say ... but what we say ...'

Worldview/view of nature

Primary:	Economic orientation: atmosphere a global public good; rich countries that damage it should pay for the damage.
Secondary:	World system is unequal; environmental agreements perpetuate inequality.

Action(s) proposed

Primary:	'Rights-based approach in regulating climate change; treating the atmosphere as a limited common resource to be managed under an equity regime based on per capita entitlements (freezing the per capita entitlements on the basis of a population distribution index for a chosen year).'
Secondary:	'Surplus entitlements with less polluting countries can give way to an international emission trading regime. An international tax can be levied on countries exceeding the limits imposed by their permissible entitlement allocation' (using the polluter pays principle).

Note: See www.earthscan.co.uk/dcc for a first-stage analysis of each of the 100 arguments.

countries and (2) excessive consumption of energy and materials, with high production of wastes, in rich countries'. His proposed solutions differ, however, from those of Agarwal and Narain in being broader in scope – control population growth, reduce the use of fossil-fuel-based energy and redistribute wealth to poor countries.

Agarwal and Narain's argument is from definition: climate change is not an unequal-business-as-usual case, where the North can call the shots; climate change is a pollution problem, and the industrialized countries of the North are the polluters. However, a cause-and-effect claim plays a large part in the overall argument; industrialized countries are the cause of climate change and thus should pay necessary mitigation and adaptation costs. McMichael's argument stresses the causal argument, laying the blame for climate change at the door of industrialized countries.

Family #11: Rift with Nature

Another family of arguments focuses attention on climate change as just one symptom of people's disturbed and dysfunctional relationship with the rest of nature. Other symptoms include various types of pollution, over-fishing and over-hunting, loss of various kinds of natural systems and habits, and many technological 'advances', such as genetically modified organisms. A retreat from industrialization is in order. We must 'live lightly on the land', 'respect Mother Earth' and so on. We must consider ourselves just one species on the Earth and respect the (equal) rights of other animals and plants to live and thrive. We should direct our efforts towards preserving the natural state of things. Often, these arguments are made for a broad range of environmental problems; climate change may or may not be on the list. I classified 15 of the 100 documents analysed in this study in this family. Again, these are arguments at the third and fourth stages (root causal analysis and value/meaning of the issue), which lead to calls for action quite different from those of the 'more modernization' families.

An example of this argument is Donella Meadows's depiction of Gaia's reaction to the negotiations leading to the Kyoto Protocol (see Table 5.9). Gaia is a term used by James Lovelock (1988) and others to describe the Earth as a whole organism that keeps life in balance. Meadows, an adjunct professor of environmental studies at Dartmouth College, argues that people have got it all wrong but may have a chance to fix it. She associates the natural harmony in Nature with the ethical life; she associates a human preoccupation with power and money with wrong-headedness that could spell catastrophe for them.

Speaking as Gaia, she says, 'I may have made a mistake when I evolved that two-legged, large-brained life-form. ... Deciding the composition of the atmosphere by counting up money "costs" makes as much sense as deciding whether a plane will fly by the position of a football on a field. Wrong measure. Wrong field. Wrong game.' At the end of the monologue, she says, 'Maybe that won't be necessary, though. ... The big-brains do have the capacity to see beyond power and money, see into the future, understand the fundamentals of my laws, distinguish between symbols and reality. Some of them know how many kinds of energy they can harness that don't put carbon back into the atmosphere. ... But they'd better hurry. ... I hope they do. I'm really quite fond of them.'

The argument makes a strong claim about what the appropriate role is for people as part of Nature and about the consequence (effect) of not using their big brains to see beyond power and money (cause).

Also in this family are 'deep green' and ecofeminist arguments, often made in more general terms than climate change, but explicitly including it as an example of a seriously misconceived relationship with nature.

Table 5.9 *First-step analysis of Meadows argument*

#8:	Meadows, Donella H. (1997) 'Mother Gaia reflects on the global climate conference', http://csf.colorado.edu/forums/ecofem/dec97/0009.html
Authority of speaker/writer	
Primary:	Meadows 'is an adjunct professor of environmental studies at Dartmouth College'.
Type of argument	
Primary:	'I may have made a mistake when I evolved that two-legged, large-brained life-form. … Deciding the composition of the atmosphere by counting up money 'costs' makes as much sense as deciding whether a plane will fly by the position of a football on a field. Wrong measure. Wrong field. Wrong game.'
Type of evidence	
Primary:	An imaginative monologue by Gaia.
Worldview/view of nature	
Primary:	Nature is large and still in charge. Human beings are arrogant if they think they can try to control climate and survive.
Action(s) proposed	
Primary:	'If they don't figure that out, I'm going to have to take a few million years and try to evolve a higher form of intelligence.'
Secondary:	'Maybe that won't be necessary, though. … The big-brains do have the capacity to see beyond power and money, see into the future, understand the fundamentals of my laws, distinguish between symbols and reality. Some of them know how many kinds of energy they can harness that don't put carbon back into the atmosphere. … But they'd better hurry. … I hope they do. I'm really quite fond of them.'

Note: See www.earthscan.co.uk/dcc for a first-stage analysis of each of the 100 arguments.

Family Ties?

Each of these families of arguments has its own story to tell about climate change. Are there indications in the arguments themselves that the gaps between families can be bridged? Or has each tribe staked out a position from which there can be little communication, trade or marriage? We can make a preliminary examination of commonalities among the families here, with a more in-depth study to come in the next chapter.

- First, all the families – representing most of the national governments of the world, thousands of scientists, environmental organizations at every level and countless others – take the question of climate change seriously, and none rules the prospect out completely.
- Second, all agree that vast uncertainties exist. Some claim that uncertainty is a reason to wait and see, others that uncertainty is a reason to act as quickly as possible.
- Third, almost all agree that climate change is not a problem *sui generis*. Socio-economic factors are involved in the industrialization that may be causing climate change, in the feasibility of reducing emissions of greenhouse gases and in the potential for adaptation to climate change. Development (or lack thereof) is an issue; the credibility of science, especially scientific models, is another. Even the argument that climate change is not a problem of *climate* locates a problem in political issues.

- Fourth, they all argue from definition, although some arguments also include cause-and-effect arguments.

These elements provide only a tenuous basis for coming to agreement. The voices in the debate agree that climate change is an issue worth serious discussion and that the definitions and the context matter in that discussion. When we look at most, instead of all, argument-makers, we see more bases (not surprisingly). Although some have hard-and-fast positions, most show their awareness of other arguments besides their own and the need to deal with, even accommodate, those arguments. In more than half of the documents, the debaters specifically refer to international processes (primarily the UNFCCC and the Intergovernmental Panel on Climate Change) and clearly consider these processes as having some authority – that is, the debate can be mediated by formal, organizational coordination and negotiation within the framework of international agreements. Most accept and use scientific evidence. The debate thus continues with an expectation (or at least a hope) of coming to agreement through the process of argumentation. The next chapter focuses on single features of the arguments as possible ties within and among families.

References

Lovelock, J. (1988) *The Ages of Gaia: A Biography of Our Living Earth*, Oxford University Press, Oxford, UK

Wallerstein, I. (1974) *The Modern World-System*, Academic Press, New York

Wallerstein, I. (1983) *Historical Capitalism, with Capitalist Civilization*, Verso, London

WCED (World Commission on Environment and Development) (1987) *Our Common Future*, Oxford University Press, Oxford, UK

6

Elements of Arguments
as Social Links

The 'family' categories demonstrate the extent of the climate change debate – and it occupies quite a bit of space, all the way from religious arguments about the 'right' relationship between people and nature to the worth of scientific evidence to the inequalities among nations, and far beyond. Once we consider scientific and non-scientific arguments together, the scope of the conversation expands considerably.

The first-stage analysis has broadened the discussion.[1] At this point we could throw up our hands and decide it's too much to handle. How can there be any agreement among people who have different assumptions, different goals and different tactics? Or – and this is where I want to go – we could perform a different type of analysis to see where there might be ties among families, social ties that might provide a basis for continuing dialogue and coming to at least partial agreements. At the end of the last chapter, I briefly touched upon a few elements, but we can do better than that.

What this chapter describes is social network analysis. In the definition given by Valdis Krebs (2007), social network analysis (SNA) is 'the mapping and measuring of relationships and flows between people, groups, organizations, computers, websites and other information/knowledge processing entities. The nodes in the network are the people and groups while the links show relationships or flows between the nodes. SNA provides both a visual and a mathematical analysis of human relationships.' Researchers often build diagrams of social networks (see the front cover of this book) so they can analyse overall patterns in the links, the density of the networks, their clusters and important cogs, and so on. Several software programs are specifically designed for these mathematical analyses.

One famous manifestation of social network analysis is evoked in the phrase 'six degrees of separation' (Watts, 2003). This is the idea that simple acquaintanceship can lead one individual to another in six links. In the original experiment, people were given a letter to a person they did not know and a task to send it to someone they knew who might either know the addressee or

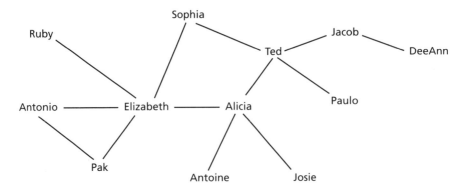

Figure 6.1 *Network of friends*

someone else who knew him. The chains that were completed in the experiment were typically six links long, hence the 'six degrees'. Such acquaintance chains are often used by job seekers (Granovetter, 1974) or those hunting for reliable contractors. For instance, if you want to find a good plumber, you might well ask your friends for a recommendation; if they can't recommend someone, they may know another person who has had a recent good experience with a plumber. *Voila!* You've networked your way to a competent plumber.

Our social networks are thus made up of people we know, well or not so well, and they connect to other networks by people who know others that we don't know. Thus I have something in common with many people I don't know, because they and I know the same person. Figure 6.1 shows a theoretical network of friends and friends of friends. The diagram shows six people I don't know personally but who know people I know.

So far I have described social networks on the basis of acquaintance or friendship – a link that is pretty obvious. But social networks can also be formed out of things-in-common, such as jobs, educational status, social class, marriage and beliefs. At social gatherings, a typical get-to-know-someone strategy is to ask where a person lives, what he or she does for a living or how he or she knows the host. The hope is that the answers will provide common ground for conversation. When the conversational gambits succeed, social links are formed.

In this chapter, I will treat the elements of arguments as social links, as things that different debaters have in common. For instance, if two or more people are university professors, they have a link (similar training, the university context, career incentives and so on). Even if two professors immediately begin arguing, their common terms and concepts link them. If two or more people lean heavily on quantitative data as evidence, they are linked by the assumptions that such evidence is valid and persuasive. They might argue about whose numbers are better, but they both think the answers will be contained in *some* numbers. If two or more people believe that it's a dog-eat-dog world out there, they are linked by assumptions about how things ought to be (for example one has to be tough to survive). Finally, if two or more people propose the same action, they are linked by a belief in the efficacy and/or rightness of that action.

For 100 documents and multiple elements, it only makes sense to code the elements so their linkages become readily apparent and can be mapped by a software program – an almost impossible task for a researcher working without such electronic assistance. The elements and the codes I used are as follows:

- argument family (FAM);
- professional authority (AU);
- organizational authority (OR);
- type of evidence (EV);
- worldview/view of nature (WV); and
- proposed actions (AC).

Each of these elements has the potential for many different expressions or subcategories; for instance, a person could have the professional authority (AU) of a scientist (AUSCI), a government official (AUPOL), a representative of industry (AUTRA) and so on. The most obvious example of diverse subcategories is Proposed Actions; many writers or speakers propose several actions. Each of these needed to have a code assigned. However, I did not pre-decide the codes but rather described and grouped those I saw in the documents.

In order to look for such links, I classified each of the argument elements and gave code names to categories within the elements. For instance, all debaters who were university faculty members were given the code AUACA: AU for author and ACA for academic. The code allows the computer program (and us) to easily group all the AUACAs. The complete list of codes is given in the annex to this chapter (page 95).

When a document is completely coded, it can be compressed to a line in a spreadsheet, like the line below for the document written by Ashford and Castelden:

ASHFOR   FAM03   AUSCI   ORNGO   EVDAT   WVECN   ACEDU   ACMON   ACRCH

Decoding this line yields the information that the document written by Ashford and Castelden (ASHFOR) is in Family 3 (FAM03) (focusing on scientific knowledge), the authors are scientists (AUSCI) who work for a non-governmental organization (ORNGO). They use data as evidence (EVDAT) and express an economic worldview (WVECN). They propose three actions: educate people about the causes and impacts of climate change (ACEDU), monitor climate change impacts (ACMON) and conduct further research (ACRCH). (The list of document-specific codes is given in Appendix 1, and the whole list of documents, by family, is in Appendix 2.)

An individual document such as that written by Ashford and Castleden illustrates the power of comparing arguments and their elements. Let's now take a closer look.

If the clamour of the debate is such that we should despair of agreement, we would expect to find that families of arguments have much internal agreement (that is, family members are pretty much all alike) but little external agreement (that is, they disagree with members of other families on most or all points). However, this is not the case.

As we might more realistically expect, individuals, including Ashford and Castleden, tend to have close ties with fellow members of their argument families, but they frequently have multiple ties outside their families. For example, Ashford and Castleden are members of Family 3, 'Science Provides Knowledge about Climate Change', which has a total of nine members. (Again, each document counts as a member.) Like many other family members, they are scientists (six documents in the family), use data and models as evidence (five members total), and advocate education, monitoring and research (seven members advocate one or more of these).

However, in the other 99 documents, there are 36 other scientists, spread out across all other families; 43 speakers/writers, again, spread out across all other families, use data and/or models as evidence; and there are 20 instances of one or more proposed actions that Ashford and Castleden also propose, spread out across eight other families.

In summary, the Ashford and Castleden partnership has many social network ties within the argument family but also many ties with debaters in other argument families. Their set of things-in-common is extensive, providing a basis for partial agreement and further discussion with members of all other families.

What are the practical implications of having so many social network ties? For participants in the debate like Ashford and Castleden, who advocate non-aggressive and relatively low-cost actions, the existence of these links could prompt them to:

- Explicitly *associate* their arguments with those made in other families – for example, in pointing out the necessity for education, monitoring and research to accomplish the more aggressive goals of the 'More Modernization' arguments;
- Demonstrate how their evidence and other types of evidence – and results from other models and data – can reinforce each other; and
- Provide additional arguments, at the first and second stases, about the need to study and monitor in order to establish whether or not something has happened and, if so, whether or not that something can be defined as climate change.

Social network analysis allows us to map these kinds of links among all 100 of the climate change debaters. From setting an individual document (for example

Ashford and Castleden) in the context of links with other participants in the debate, we will discuss within-family links, then (using a software program) examine the strength of links among the 100 speakers/writers regardless of their family affiliations. But first comes the question, why do we expect that similar elements will really link disparate people? Discussing the elements in more depth will help answer that question.

Authority of the Speaker/Writer and Organization Type

The credentials and standing of the writer and his or her organization are likely to influence the audience's reception of the argument. As it is impossible to make an objective judgment about how respected a writer is, I have chosen to characterize the writers of the 100 documents by their professional positions: scientist, policymaker/government official, member of an NGO (typically an organization in the environmental social movement), representative of a trade association or leader of a business, or faculty member at a college or university. Almost the same categories apply to the organization type, with the addition of 'church' as a type of organization. (None of the writers was identified as a church professional.)

Audiences expect that the authority of the writer and organization will vary according to type. People normally credit *scientists* with understanding the technical bases for belief (or denial) that activities of humans are affecting the global climate; scientists also share professional backgrounds and the use of defined (scientific) methods. *Policymakers and government officials* have certain responsibilities for ensuring the wellbeing of citizens, along with incentives for elected officials to demonstrate benefits within their terms of office. *Nongovernmental organization (NGO) members* typically are actively working against the status quo on behalf of the environment and/or people who are seen as the victims of its degradation. They may use inflammatory or extreme language – or publicity-seeking actions – to make their points. *Trade organization and business people* can be seen, especially by NGO members, as against anything that will reduce profits, such as installing extra equipment to prevent emissions of carbon dioxide. Universities and their *faculty members* are supposed to have a more disinterested view of things, on the one hand; but on the other hand they can be seen as impractical ('ivory tower') in their conclusions and proposals for action. *Church-based speakers* may have built-in biases towards a stewardship ethic and against consumerist lifestyles; audiences may discount what they say by citing these biases.

Moreover, the type of speaker/writer and type of organization provide a way of linking people in a sub-network, for example on the basis of their scientific backgrounds or environmental advocacy or industry affiliation. Authority characteristics are thus proxies for social network ties.

Type of Evidence

Evidence is what backs up an argument. Thus evidence can include not only facts and numbers but also logic, stories and compelling images. Speakers/writers use at least 12 types of evidence, listed in no particular order in the annex to this chapter: historical evidence, scientific literature (as citations/references), rights-based arguments, utilitarianism or economic evidence, case studies, anecdotes/personal stories, data and computerized models, theory, expert testimony, political analysis, metaphor, and pictures. For each document, I distinguished up to three types of evidence, basing the categorizations on my judgment of what 'carries' the argument. (Again, I did not set three as an upper limit; this was the maximum of types I found in a single document.) Many types of scientific writing are metaphorical, for example, but, if the writer obviously intends the data to authorize his or her argument, the document evidence was categorized as 'data and computerized models'.

Historical arguments are generally of two types. The writer may explain the history of views of nature and shifts in how nature is perceived. Or the document may contain a history of the political response to climate change, perhaps beginning with the debates leading to the 1992 Rio Summit and the Framework Convention on Climate Change, then discussing the subsequent Conferences of the Parties and the politics of these negotiations.

If a writer uses *scientific literature-based evidence*, the attempt is to gather the authorities that exist to attest to the truth of what is being said. In its simplest form, this can be statements that begin, 'Scientists agree that …'. Its more complex forms use technical citation methods to array studies that provide backing for the current argument, as when a scientific article's first sentence contains dozens of citations. This latter use of scientific evidence places the writer in the company of supposedly learned people, to be considered one of the company.

Rights-based arguments rely on logical or philosophical implications of the assertion that people have equal rights. US writers, assuming agreement that people have equal rights under the law, may test that assumption by gathering data on the social class of those tried and convicted of various crimes. For the case of climate change, a debater may claim that all people in the world have rights to clean air or rights to emit greenhouse gases. Under the equal-rights principle, people in highly industrialized countries are then encroaching on the rights of people in less industrialized countries, and the latter group has just as much right to emit greenhouse gases as the former group.

Utilitarian/economic arguments, on the other hand, assert the principle of the greatest good for the greatest number. The world as a whole will be better off, one argument goes, if reducing emissions starts with the cheap actions, then moves to more expensive actions. Thus equality of rights is not a consideration, although 'winners' are supposed to compensate 'losers'.

Rights-based and utilitarian/economic arguments are often seen as opposed. The former type insists on every individual's rights to, among other things, clean air and stable climate. Rights-based arguments are often opposed on principle to averaging and the perpetuation of inequality; thus, debaters from the global South often use rights-based arguments. Utilitarian arguments attempt to provide the most clean air and stable climate to most people – to maximize the greatest good to the greatest number – while recognizing that there will be winners and losers (and that winners will need to compensate losers). Averages, normal curves and the use of existing unequal institutions are the stock-in-trade of economist utilitarians, who are often identified with debaters from the global North.

Case studies are commonly used in rights-based arguments, but can be used in other arguments as well. Cases are typically analysed at a country or sub-national level – for example, a case study of how six developing countries have slowed the growth of emissions in their countries. Case studies differ from *personal or anecdotal evidence* in that the former is more rigorously and self-consciously scientific, where the latter is manifestly a retelling of one person's experience; case studies can be used to develop theory that may be applied to other cases. Anecdotes try to capture a 'truth' about climate change or to persuade an audience who will be moved to sympathize with the plight, for example, of a Bangladeshi who must choose to save only one of two children in a flood.

Data and computerized models are likely to be used in utilitarian or cost–benefit arguments. They provide sources of evidence about rising concentrations of greenhouse gases and their effects on climate. So it is not surprising to find elaborate data tables and models used extensively in arguments about climate change, with regard not only to the physics and chemistry of climate change but also to emissions-producing human activities and international negotiations about the issue.

Sometimes an argument is *pure theory* – about relationships between human beings and non-human nature, about modernization and its effects, about globalization and climate change, about ecofeminist attitudes towards environmental damage, and so on. Social theorists, although typically making much broader arguments, may include climate change as an example of a global problem that demonstrates the theoretical argument.

Debaters may call upon *experts* to give testimony about climate change, as experts do about other issues. A few arguments consist largely of a string of quotations, direct and indirect, from people in positions of authority.

Political analysis can be the principal evidence for an argument, as when neo-institutionalists argue that climate change is a unique problem for policy-makers, necessitating different institutions than the ones the world has.

Explicitly *metaphorical arguments* can speak directly to certain audiences. One example in this set of documents is the use of the Gaia metaphor (Gaia being the principle of self-regulation in the Earth system, as described by James Lovelock, 1988). This document, discussed in the previous chapter, pictures Gaia as a woman talking about where people have gone wrong and what they might be able to do to avoid extinction.

Only one document in this set primarily uses *pictures* to make an argument about how climate is changing around the globe. However, other documents include pictures to 'bring home' their messages of ecological damage, for example from sea level rise.

Worldview

A writer's worldview, especially related to the relationship between human beings and non-human nature, may constitute the main argument, or it may remain largely implicit in the argument. Either way, his or her worldview permeates the choices of argument, evidence and proposed actions. In the first chapter, a family's worldview was spoken of as a shared starting point for debate. If family members agree that family loyalty and solidarity are important, then a member's arguing that he or she would rather spend time with his or her friends than go on a family vacation is ruled out of bounds. If, on the other hand, the family is valued as an incubator of independent individuals, then such an argument might be welcomed.

This set of documents exhibits nine worldviews:

1   *Economic*, the view that nature is a storehouse of scarce resources that must be accounted for. In this worldview, everything has costs and benefits; when society has done this calculation, it will know what to do – the choice that has the most net benefits.
2   *Moral*, the view that people have (but do not necessarily enjoy) equal rights to use natural resources. In this worldview, individual rights are more important than the 'common good'. Even if society as a whole will be better off under certain conditions, it does not have the right to disadvantage individuals.
3   *Ecocentric*, the view that plants, animals and indeed geographical features have the same rights to exist and be healthy that human beings have. In this worldview, people may not interfere with natural processes, the lives of plants and animals, and so on, beyond what is necessary for survival.
4   *Ecomodern*, the view that people can improve the efficiency of their uses of natural resources. In this worldview, societies can manage natural processes – and improve their management if they learn that there are unintended negative consequences. Specifically, if energy-producing technologies have turned out to be contributing to climate change by emitting greenhouse gases, new technologies need to be invented that do not emit greenhouse gases.
5   *Political*, the view that changes in Nature are the direct result of political actions, and that therefore politics should be the primary focus on environmentalist efforts. In this worldview, the primary issue is how to set up an agreed-on regime to control emissions of greenhouse gases; thus negotiation of this regime is always the first task.

6 *Cautious*, respectful or alarmist because nature is fragile, unknowable or of an unknown finite 'carrying capacity'. In this worldview, people should not disturb nature unless they know they will not harm it – the precautionary principle.

7 *Constructivist*, the view that social ideas of nature determine our treatment of and response to nature. In this worldview, the most important element is not the physical reality of nature but the meanings people assign to it (for example as provider of energy and food or as transcendent beauty). Thus climate change is the result of people thinking about nature in incorrect ways.

8 *Confident* that nature is robust and will survive anything that human beings can do to it. This worldview stresses the resilience and autonomy of nature, which cannot be changed by any puny efforts people make.

9 *Religious*, the view that people have been designated as 'stewards' of natural resources and thus should use them cautiously and with care for their health. In this worldview, God (or a god-like organizing principle) wants people to live in harmony with nature.

Proposed Actions

Within this set of documents are 31 proposed actions, sometimes espoused singly, sometimes in combination with others. They are listed in a very abbreviated form in the chapter annex; below they are listed in a more comprehensible fashion:

1 All countries (and other entities) should reduce emissions of greenhouse gases, particularly from fossil fuel use, but also from activities involving methane, nitrous oxide and other greenhouse gases.

2 Those who have polluted the atmosphere with greenhouse gases should pay for remediation, by compensating those who will be negatively affected by climate change, investing in ways to reduce emissions or both.

3 'Contraction and convergence' is the term used to describe a strategy of focusing on reducing global emission permits while establishing a universally applied individual emissions allowance, and working to have industrialized and non-industrialized countries converge on that allowance.

4 Industrialized countries should reduce emissions immediately, but non-industrialized countries should be allowed to develop economically first.

5 Zero- or low-emitting technologies should be developed, especially in the areas of power generation.

6 The Kyoto Protocol should be implemented.

7 An emissions trading system should be implemented, to reduce the cost of mitigation.

8 Climate change policies should be integrated with other policies, for example in improving human wellbeing.

9   Countries and individuals should prepare to adapt to climate change.
10 'Carbon sinks' should be developed to capture and store carbon dioxide rather than releasing it to the atmosphere.
11 People should return to a simpler lifestyle in order not to affect the climate.
12 Controlling population growth will control climate change.
13 Equality among nations will allow us to deal with climate change.
14 We should build sustainable systems (joining climate change and sustainability issues).
15 The balance between human beings and nature should be restored.
16 The most affected people should be assisted.
17 People should be educated about the causes and impacts of climate change.
18 The impacts of climate change should be monitored.
19 We should create desirable scenarios of the future and work towards them.
20 Both mitigation and adaptation projects should be supported/funded.
21 We should focus on 'no regrets' activities, in other words those that would be good to do even if climate does not change.
22 Scientists should do more research to understand the causes and impacts of climate change.
23 We can understand the prospects of climate change by examining how climate has changed in the past and societal responses to the changes.
24 We should do nothing – climate change is not a problem.
25 Government incentives should be revised to reward, for example, actions to improve energy efficiency.
26 Scientists should improve their models of climate change, impacts and so on.
27 Industry should be engaged in the effort to reduce emissions.
28 Because much is uncertain, we should use an act–learn–act approach.
29 We should cap per capita emissions.
30 We should grow the world's economies; rich economies can mitigate or adapt to climate change, as well as other types of change.
31 The international negotiations should continue.

Within-Family Analysis

A close examination of the documents and codes demonstrates that the rhetorical elements of authority, evidence and worldview do indeed link members of families. That is, families seem to be dominated by certain categories of individuals and organizations, by the evidence they use and by worldview. But proposed actions, the fourth category, do not seem to be links within families.

Authority provides within-family links; however, the kinds of speakers/writers and organizations in the climate change debate as a whole constitute a limited set. Scientists are the most prominent members in all families except Family #11 (where academics predominate), Family #2 (three non-attributions, two trade association representatives, two academics and a scientist) and Family #4 (two of the eight members are scientists and two are environmental advocates; the rest are single types). Environmental advocates have substantive voices in Families #5, #9 and #10. The other part of authority, organization types, provides some – but not overwhelming – coherence, as seen in the list below:

- Family #1   3 total – 3 universities;
- Family #2   8 total – 4 NGOs;
- Family #3   9 total – 3 government, 3 research organizations;
- Family #4   8 total – 6 NGOs;
- Family #5   10 total – 4 government, 4 NGOs;
- Family #6   10 total – 5 NGOs, 2 research organizations;
- Family #7   4 total – 3 government;
- Family #8   5 total – 2 non-attributions, rest single types;
- Family #9   10 total – 6 NGOs, 3 government, 3 universities;
- Family #10 18 total – 9 NGOs, 3 government, 3 universities;
- Family #11 15 total – 7 universities, 5 NGOs.

The predominant *types of evidence* used by all families except #10 and #11 are data and scientific literature; this is in keeping with the dominance of scientists as participants in the debate. Family #10 exhibits a wide range of evidence types, with most debaters using two or more types; political analysis (seven uses), data (six uses), rights-based evidence (four uses), scientific literature (four uses) and history (three uses) are the most frequent types in this family. Family #11 members have a smaller range of frequently used evidence types: scientific literature (six uses), metaphor (four uses), history (four uses) and anecdote/personal testimony (three uses).

Common *worldviews* provide the most coherence within families:

- As expected, in Families #5–9 (who all espouse More Modernization) an ecomodern worldview predominates; Family #4, also a pro-modernization family, has three instances of an ecomodern worldview and five instances of a political worldview.
- Two members of Family #1 and three members of Family #2 hold the view that nature is robust; the remaining Family #1 member holds a political worldview, and in Family #2 three other members hold an economic worldview and the remaining two hold an ecomodern worldview.
- Three-quarters of Family #10 members hold moral, nature-as-fragile or political worldviews, in keeping with the focus on inequality.
- Almost all Family #11 members hold ecocentric, nature-as-fragile or social constructivist worldviews.

No such coherence can be found in the *actions proposed* by family members. Proposed actions are not clustered in families, with a few exceptions: Family #1 members all propose no action; five (of eight) members of Family #2 and seven (of 10) members of Family #5 propose technology solutions; and six (of

10) members of Family #6 and seven (of 10) members of Family #9 propose emissions reductions. Especially when one considers that speakers/writers proposed up to five actions, this lack of agreement within families is striking.

What does this tell us about the participants in the broad debate and about how debaters are linked?

The participants include a large proportion of scientists. Although this non-random sample only suggests the dominance of science, other evidence strengthens this suggestion; the prominent role of research and researchers shows up in almost everyone's arguments, using scientific results to bolster their arguments or to discredit other arguments. The well-known movie *An Inconvenient Truth*, for instance, rests on science and was widely discussed on its scientific merits.

Beyond the inescapability of science, we can note that there seem to be two groupings: the 'more modernization' families (#5–9), as expected, have quite a bit in common, notably the types of evidence used and their worldviews. Families #10 and #11 (concerned with inequality and the rights of nature) also cohere in certain ways: a wider variety of types of evidence (much less emphasis on data) and worldviews that tend towards the perception of nature as fragile.

Yet the negative possibility that arguments about climate change are walled off from each other, effectively precluding agreement, is clearly *not* the case. Those participating in the debate have much in common with others making the same general argument – but also many elements in common with others outside their argument 'families'.

In order to go beyond this analysis and get a sense of network ties among individuals, regardless of their family affiliations, I turn to software-assisted social network analysis in the next chapter.

Note

1 See www.earthscan.co.uk/dcc for a first-stage analysis of each of the 100 arguments considered in this book.

References

Granovetter, M. (1974) *Getting a Job*, University of Chicago Press, Chicago, IL
Krebs, V. (2007) 'Social network analysis, an introduction', www.orgnet.com/sna.html
Lovelock, J. (1988) *The Ages of Gaia: A Biography of Our Living Earth*, Oxford University Press, Oxford, UK
Watts, D. (2003) *Six Degrees: The Science of a Connected Age*, Norton, New York

Annex: Argument elements that may form social ties

Name of Variable	Value	Code
Document #		1–100
Argument Family	Climate change is not a problem	FAM01
	Climate change could be good for people	FAM02
	Science can solve the problem of climate change	FAM03
	Modernization – policy is the key	FAM04
	Modernization – reform the energy system	FAM05
	Modernization – focus on mitigation	FAM06
	Modernization – focus on adaptation	FAM07
	Modernization – economics can find efficient solutions	FAM08
	Modernization – mitigation and adaptation are both important	FAM09
	Reduce inequality in order to deal with climate change	FAM10
	Worldviews must alter to 'back to nature' or accord nature rights	FAM11
Professional Authority		
	Scientist	AUSCI
	Policymaker/government official	AUSPOL
	Representative of a non-governmental organization (NGO)	AUENV
	Representative of a trade association/business	AUTRA
	Academic	AUACA
Organizational Authority		
	Research	ORRES
	Government	ORGOV
	NGO	ORNGO
	Trade association	ORIND
	Business	ORBSS
	University	ORUNI
	Church	ORCHU
Type of evidence		
	Historical	EVHIS
	Scientific/literature citations and discussion	EVSCT
	Rights-based	EVRIT
	Utilitarian/economic	EVUTI
	Case studies	EVCAS
	Anecdotes/personal testimony	EVANE
	Data-based/models	EVDAT
	Theory	EVTHE
	Experts' opinions	EVEXP
	Political analysis	EVPAN
	Metaphor	EVMET
	Pictures	EVPIX
Worldview/view of nature		
	Economic	WVECN
	Moral/inequality	WVMOR
	Ecocentric	WVECO
	Ecomodernism	WVMOD
	Political	WVPLY
	Nature fragile/unknowable/finite carrying capacity	WVNAT
	Social construction	WVSCO
	Nature robust	WVROB
	Religious/stewardship ethic	WVREL

Proposed actions

	Reduce emissions/fossil fuel use	ACEMI
	Polluter pays	ACPAY
	Contraction and convergence	ACCNC
	Industrialized countries mitigate first, while developing countries develop	ACDIF
	Better technology	ACTEC
	Implement Kyoto	ACKYO
	Emissions trading	ACETR
	Integrate climate change policies with other policies	ACINT
	Prepare to adapt	ACADA
	Develop sinks	ACSNK
	Back to nature/simple lifestyle	ACBAC
	Control population growth	ACPOP
	Work towards equality	ACEQU
	Build sustainability	ACSUS
	Restore human/nature balance	ACRST
	Assist most affected people	ACAFF
	Educate	ACEDU
	Monitor impacts	ACIPM
	Work backward from scenarios	ACSCE
	Fund mitigation/adaptation projects	ACFND
	'No regrets'	ACNRG
	Do more research	ACRCH
	Use history to understand	ACHST
	Do nothing	ACZER
	Revise government incentives	ACINC
	Improve models	ACMDL
	Engage industry	ACEGA
	Act–learn–act	ACALA
	Cap per capita emissions	ACPCE
	Grow economies	ACGRO
	Continue international negotiations	ACNEG
Year	1991–2003	Y1991– Y2003

7

Beyond Family Ties: Social Network Analysis

Inside and outside our families, we all have interlocking and overlapping social networks, based on mutual activities, types or locations of jobs, schools or other past experiences, children's (or parents') friends, churches, clubs, neighbourhoods, and so on. Dense and overlapping networks are associated with healthy civil societies. Conversely, the absence of network ties may be a sign of something societally amiss, as Robert Putnam noted in his well-known book *Bowling Alone* (Putnam, 2000). Putnam, who has shown that Italian states whose people have strong associative ties (churches, social clubs and other organizations) also exhibit high economic performance (Putnam, 1993), discusses in *Bowling Alone* the decline of such associative ties in the US. Particularly important are ties that overlap; for instance, I could interact with someone by being in the same bridge club and also shop in the store that she owns, while a fellow customer might have a child who is friends at school with her child, and so on.

In the study I am detailing here, I have defined a limited set of ties, so I am nowhere near capturing the potential ties among these 100+ people (counting co-authors). (Other types of ties might include attendance at the same meetings, provision of information, co-authorship of papers or participating in other global debates. In other social network studies, holding directorates on corporate boards or donating money to political candidates also constitute ties, as well as personal friendship or marriage ties.) Nevertheless, the first part of this social network analysis – straightforward grouping into argument families, coding and first-order inspection – suggested that participants have things in common. This is so even though the climate change debate may seem to be marked by sharp disagreements and strident language.

This chapter extends the analysis to find out *how many* links the individuals in this debate have to each other. That is, each of the 100+ debaters may have a potential of at least five ties to any other debater: profession, organization type, preferred evidence, worldview and proposed actions. We know that a family tends to have many internal ties, but now we want to know whether,

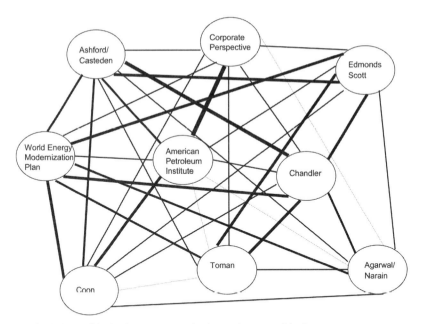

Note: The thickness of the line between two nodes denotes how many links there are.

Figure 7.1 *Social network ties: Group 1a*

leaving aside family ties, individuals (as authors of documents) are linked in multiple ways to others.

In order to do this, I put all the debaters on the same footing (minus their family/argument affiliations) and asked the software program to create groups based on how many links could be found among the individuals. I can use Ashford and Castleden as an example again. No longer am I trying to see how they are connected to family members or by single ties to debaters outside their family. Instead, I am trying to find out how they are linked to 99+ others, regardless of their main arguments in the climate change debate. Theoretically, Ashford and Castleden could have more social network ties to people outside their family than inside. Do they? And how about everybody else?

Looking for the maximum number of ties between people, UCINET (a social network analysis program developed by Steve Borgatti of Analytic Technologies) partitioned the 100 debaters into four groups. Three are fairly even in size (35, 30 and 31 members), and these are further divided into three or four subgroups. The fourth group has only four members.

Ashford and Castleden were placed in Group 1a, which has nine members. The one element all members of this group have in common is an economic worldview – that is, the worldview that everything has costs and benefits. Beyond this common link, this group tends to look like a friendship network, with multiple overlapping ties, as Figure 7.1 shows. Except for three single links, pairs have at least two links, with the largest number of links (six) between two corporatist organizations.

Again, these are only a few of the elements that people have in common; in addition, they may actually know each other, attend the same meetings or workshops, co-author or read each other's papers, and so on. They may be talking, face to face or via email or phone. In any case, more likely than not, they are aware of other arguments being made in the debate.

Finally, these nine documents and nine-plus authors are derived from five different argument families (#2 'Climate Change Could Be Good for You', #3 'Science Provides Knowledge about Climate Change', #5 'Reform the Energy System', #8 'Get the Prices Right' and #11 'Inequality Is the Problem'). So although the arguments people make are important, worldview may be a more important tie, and combinations of ties do not coincide with family membership. Emphasizing worldview, then, or a combination of tics as yet unspecified, may hold the potential to allow a process of debate that can build at least partial agreements among debaters.

Group 1a may be the only group that's so linked with overlapping ties, since it is the first group formed by UCINET, but it would be tedious to go through all 12 subgroups, and with large groups the networks are simply too dense to make sense of visually. (For those interested, the Annex to this chapter on page 104 shows, in shorthand, the groups and the individual attributes of the group members.) But we can look at a middle group and the last, perhaps quirky, four-person group, Group 4. It may be that groups get less linked as the program goes along and the four people at the end are outliers or leftovers.

Group 2c is a middle group with 19 members. (I've omitted a diagram showing the ties because it looks like the proverbial spaghetti bowl.) The members all have in common worldview – the worldview that nature is fragile and that we do not know when we might be doing permanent damage or crossing some threshold that can't be undone. In this worldview, people need to be very careful about interfering with natural processes. In its implications, the worldview is very different from the economic worldview of Group 1a. There, although economic theory recognizes that resources are scarce (in other words limited), in practice resources simply get more expensive the scarcer they get and substitutes can be found when resources run out. If nature is seen as fragile, however, the first questions people should ask are not 'How much does it cost and are we willing to pay?' but rather 'Can we be sure we are not damaging nature in some irremediable way?' We will come back to this point.

In this group, family membership is not nearly as scattered as it was in Group 1a. Again, there are five families represented – but among more than double the group members. Moreover, Families #9 ('Mitigate and Adapt'), #10 ('Inequality Is the Problem') and #11 ('Rift with Nature') predominate. Four of the group come from Family #9, four from Family #10 and seven from Family #11 – a total of 15 of the 19 in the group. Two of the group are from Family #6 ('Mitigate Climate Change') and one each from Family #5 ('Reform the Energy System') and Family #8 ('Get the Prices Right').

This is interesting for two reasons. First, the group shows greater family solidarity in that worldviews line up with argument families more than in the first group put together by the software. This probably means that other ties are more important in Group 1a than they are in this group. Second, even in this more homogeneous group (at least in terms of family membership), two members of Group 2c come from families that are also represented in Group 1a. Members of these two families could thus be seen as bridging two world-views that look very incompatible. In other words, connections might be made even in the most unlikely ways.

To see whether this is the case, let us look more closely at the candidate 'bridgers' from Families #5 and #8. In Group 1a, they are the World Energy Modernization Plan from Family #5 and Michael Toman and Jae Edmonds/Michael Scott from Family #8. In Group 2c, they are the German Advisory Council from Family #5 and Eugene Linden from Family #8. How can these family members make similar arguments but espouse very different worldviews?

In Family #5, the World Energy Modernization Plan and the German Advisory Council both focus on the overhaul of the world's energy system and suggest many of the same strategies: develop technology, reduce emissions and build sustainability. The World Energy Modernization Plan adds to this list two proposed actions: work towards equality and introduce emissions trading. The German Advisory Council adds another two: fund projects and do more research. The World Energy Modernization Plan strongly focuses on human choices about which resources from Nature to use (fossil fuels or renewable and energy-efficient fuels), thus placing the plan in the context of a worldview that emphasizes the costs and benefits of alternative choices. The German Advisory Council has a dual focus on people's rights to energy and on support-ing/protecting natural systems against unsustainable use; the worldview context of a fragile Nature is thus not far from a cost/benefit analysis that also worries about sustainability. Sustainability is the concept that links what are, in the abstract, incompatible worldviews.

In Family #8, Toman and the writing team Edmonds and Scott are all economists who strongly emphasize costs and benefits of policies and other actions, thus locating themselves squarely in the economics-oriented world-view. Linden, too, discusses the costs of the US policy of doing nothing: weather-related and insurance losses, which should prompt businesses to rethink their positions on climate change. Indeed, the Linden article is titled 'Who's going to pay for climate change?'. But here the emphasis is on the worldview that Nature is fragile as the reason why impacts will be large. Where Toman, Edmonds and Scott are discussing risks, Linden is speaking of what he feels are virtual certainties. The economic language provides the bridge between the two worldviews.

We are leaving some loose ends to be tied up later, but, first, we'll look at the smallest group of the computer-aided social network analysis: Group 4, with four members.

Far from being a group of 'leftovers' or 'misfits', Group 4 exhibits strong, multiple linkages. They are all scientists, all use data as evidence and all share

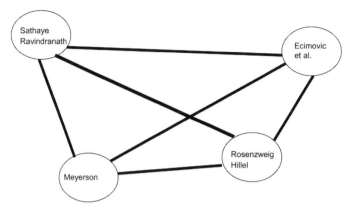

Figure 7.2 *Social network ties: Group 4a*

two worldviews: the ecomodern view that people can manage problems in Nature and the view that people must be cautious because Nature is fragile (see Figure 7.2). Even their families are close: one 'Science Provides Knowledge about Climate Change' (#3), two 'Mitigate Climate Change' (#6) and one 'Prepare to Adapt' (#7). These families are science- and technology-oriented, middle-of-the-road arguments (with 'No Problem!' at one end of the spectrum and 'Rift with Nature' at the other end). With this much in common, we would expect that their proposed actions would be similar, but there we would be wrong. They have not a proposal in common. Here are the four sets of proposed actions:

1 Control population, reduce per capita emissions;
2 Take 'no regrets' actions;
3 Build sustainability and continue to negotiate; and
4 Prepare to adapt and act–learn–act.

From Group 1a we learned that we can't predict the argument from the world-view; from Group 4 we can learn that we can't predict proposed actions even from science, data and worldview ties.

We could go on. Group 1b (10 members) is more diverse than 1a, linked most strongly by two worldviews, either morality or policy – and, in two cases, both worldviews, which is how members of this sub-network are linked.[1] Group 1c members (11) all express the worldview that nature is socially constructed, ten are scientists or academics and seven are affiliated with universities. Group 1d members (5) are linked by the worldview that nature is robust and (except for one) that the world should do nothing about the prospect of climate change.

Similarly, Groups 2 and 3 and their subgroups are linked most commonly by worldview: an ecological worldview (all eight members of Group 2, first subgroup), the worldview that nature is fragile/unknowable/finite (all 19 members of Group 2, third subgroup) or that nature is fragile/unknowable/finite *and* human actions are most importantly political (both members of Group 2, fourth subgroup), and the worldview that human beings can manage their environment successfully (all members of Group 3, with additional worldviews demarcating small subgroups of one and two members).

The tendency of groups to be formed around worldview can be attributed at least partially to a feature of the data. There are only nine worldview values, contrasted to 12 values for author and organization (which were considered together as constituting the authority of the writer/speaker), 12 values for evidence, and 31 values for proposed actions. Furthermore, it is not unusual to have missing values in the author and/or organization types, if these were not given in the document – but every document expressed at least one worldview. Thus it is easier to correlate documents by worldview than by any other type of variable. Even so, the linkages are remarkable.

However, as important to this study as linkages is diversity. That is, I am interested in whether speakers/writers and arguments that appear to be closed and of little influence outside their own 'families' have network ties that link them to other families. This appears to be the case, as indicated by the UCINET-assisted analysis.

Instead of looking at groups or families, we can instead look at the links themselves. For example, the actions proposed are potential ties among members of different families. There are 31 actions proposed in this set of documents; many speakers/writers propose more than one action. Some of the proposed actions, such as reducing emissions and developing new technologies, span many families, many types of debaters and many types of evidence. These links may be particularly potent bases for agreement, as is suggested by other global debates. For example, in the 1970s population debate, disparate actors joined forces because they, for different reasons, favoured a certain course of action.[2]

If debaters can agree on one or more actions they wish to see taken, they may be able to put aside (or at least table) their different worldviews or evidence in order to agree on a course of action to address climate change. For example, the recommendation to develop new technologies to address climate change is made by members of eight different families – only the arguments 'Science Provides Knowledge about Climate Change', 'More Modernization Is the Cure (Economics)' and 'Rift with Nature' documents contain no pro-technology arguments. Similarly, proposals for new technologies span six of the nine worldviews (all except moral/inequality, ecocentric and social construction).

Conclusion

Here's some of what we can learn overall from this exercise in social network analysis. Social network analysis of arguments demonstrates, like the analysis in the chapter on globalization, that there are both many different facets involved in the debate – differences in arguments, authority, evidence, worldview and proposals – but also a multitude of ways that people can connect, both minor and major. The social network analysis revealed multiple links within and across 'families' of arguments, thus providing potential bases for agreements.

The previous chapter gave an example of how this could work if individuals chose to emphasize the points of agreement among elements of their argument and elements of other arguments. To reiterate that point, Ashford and Castleden could demonstrate how their (Family #3) science solutions also benefit the more technical solutions found in Families #4–8 and how their evidence reinforces other evidence.

To take another example, one not included in this analysis, Aubrey Meyer takes this tack in advocating 'contraction and convergence'. This is the idea that each person should get an allowance of greenhouse gas emissions; at first, wealthy country citizens would get a larger allowance than citizens of poorer countries, but eventually the allowances would converge to one amount, which would contract to the level commensurate with climate stabilization. What Meyer does (in a steady stream of emails and on his website) is to point to statements made by others that either explicitly or implicitly refer to this idea. Thus over time he has developed a very long list of people who agree with contraction and convergence.

Institutions, of course, could also adopt a strategy of emphasizing points of agreement among the elements of their arguments and elements of arguments that others have made. In looking at the strength of the ties around institutional reports, I suspect that this is exactly what is happening. In assembling author teams and citing a large number of research and reports, the institutional report brings together a number of arguments based on things-in-common.

In a sense, this chapter ends with the question asked at the beginning: If there are many points of connection, even agreement – and if the potential exists for people to emphasize these points of connection – why is it that many disagreements persist? Perhaps the answer lies not in the potential for agreement but in what we expect the characteristics of that agreement to be.

Notes

1 That is, any member of the subgroup can link to another; a member who holds only a morality worldview can link to another member who holds only a policy worldview via one of the members who holds both worldviews.
2 In the case of the population debate, feminists and neo-Malthusians both wanted female emancipation and education in the form of birth control programmes.

References

Putnam, R. (2000) *Bowling Alone: The Collapse and Revival of American Community*, Simon and Schuster, New York, NY
Putnam, R. (1993) *Making Democracy Work: Civic Traditions in Modern Italy*, Princeton University Press, Princeton, NJ

Annex: Groups with 'Things-in-Common' Based on Social Network Analysis

UCINET Group	Author or Title	Argument Family (number)	Authority
1a	Agarwal and Narain	Reduce inequality (10)	Environmentalists, NGO
	Chandler	Reduce inequality (10)	Scientist, NGO
	Toman	Economics (8)	Scientist
	Edmonds and Scott	Economics (8)	Scientists, NGO
	Global Warming – A Corporate Perspective	Could be good (2)	Trade organization, industry
	American Petroleum Institute	Could be good (2)	Trade organization, industry
	Coon	Could be good (2)	Academic, NGO
	World Energy Modernization Plan	Energy modernization (5)	Scientist and environmentalist, NGO
	Ashford and Castleden	Science solutions (3)	Scientist, NGO
1b	Blanchard, Criqui, Trommetter and Viguier	Political modernization (4)	NGO
	Robinson	Political modernization (4)	Government
	Müller	Reduce inequality (10)	Member of a trade organization
	Quick	Reduce inequality (10)	Church
	Boehmer-Christiansen	Reduce inequality (10)	Scientist
	Jamieson	Reduce inequality (10)	Academic, university
	Ribot	Reduce inequality (10)	Scientist, NGO and university
	Sokona, Najam and Huq	Reduce inequality (10)	Scientist, NGO
	Slade	Science solutions (3)	Policymaker, government
	Lindzen	No problem! (1)	Scientist, university
1c	Rayner and Malone	Reduce inequality (10)	Scientists, research org
	Glantz	Reduce inequality (10)	Scientist, research org and government
	Sandalow and Bowles	Political modernization (4)	Scientist, NGO and university
	Edwards	Political modernization (4)	Scientist, university
	Plumwood	Rights of nature (11)	Academic, university
	Conway, Keniston and Marx	Rights of nature (11)	Academic, university
	Worster	Rights of nature (11)	Academic, university

Evidence	Worldview	Proposed Actions
History, rights	Economic, moral	Polluters pay, cap per capita emissions
Data, expert testimony	Economic	Reduce emissions, monitor, fund projects
Utilitarian	Economic	Reduce emissions, prepare to adapt, continue to negotiate
Utilitarian, data	Economic	Emissions trading
Data	Economic	Develop technology, do nothing
Data	Economic	Develop technology, do more research, revise government incentives
Policy analysis	Economic	Develop technology, do more research
Policy analysis	Economic, policy	Develop technology, reduce emissions, emissions trading, work toward equality, build sustainability
Data	Economic	Educate, monitor, do more research
Data, rights	Policy	Reduce emissions, emissions trading, contraction and convergence, developed countries first
Expert testimony	Policy	Adopt Kyoto Protocol
Data, policy analysis	Moral, policy	Assist the most affected
Rights	Moral	Contraction and convergence, back to nature, work toward equality
Policy analysis	Policy	Continue to negotiate
History, policy analysis	Moral	Work toward equality, reduce per capita emissions
Rights, case studies	Moral	Work toward equality, use history to understand
Scientific literature	Moral, policy	Reduce emissions, work toward equality, reduce per capita emissions, continue to negotiate
History	Policy	Integrate climate change with other policy, build sustainability, no regrets, do more research
Scientific literature	Policy	Develop technology, do more research, do nothing
Anecdote, metaphor	Social construction	Integrate climate change with other policy, assist the most affected
Scientific literature, metaphor	Social construction	Educate, do more research
Scientific literature, policy analysis	Policy, social construction	Adopt Kyoto Protocol
History, data	Social construction	Improve models, act–learn–act
Anecdote	Social construction	Work toward equality, restore people–nature balance
Theory	Social construction	No regrets, use history to understand
History, metaphor	Social construction	Back to nature, restore people–nature balance, change government incentives

UCINET Group	Author or Title	Argument Family (number)	Authority
	Harré, Brockmeier and Mühlhäusler	Rights of nature (11)	Academic, university
	Van Asselt and Rotmans	Science solutions (3)	Scientists, research org
	Dessai	Mitigation plus adaptation (9)	Environmentalist, NGO
	Shove	Mitigation plus adaptation (9)	Scientist, university
1d	Greening Earth Society	Could be good (2)	NGO
	US Dept. of State	Could be good (2)	Government
	Idso and Idso	Could be good (2)	NGO
	Singer	No problem! (1)	Scientist, university
	Calder	No problem! (1)	Academic, university
2a	National Wildlife Federation	Rights of nature (11)	NGO
	Meadows	Rights of nature (11)	Academic, university
	McKibben	Rights of nature (11)	Scientist, university
	Kawashima	Energy modernization (5)	Scientist, government
	Taubes	Science solutions (3)	Research org
	Darwin, Tsigas, Lewandrowski and Raneses	Science solutions (3)	Scientist, government
	Martens, Rotmans and Niessen	Science solutions (3)	Scientist, research org
	Clean Water Action	Mitigation (6)	NGO
2b	Society, Religion and Technology Project	Mitigation (6)	Church
2c	Braasch	Mitigation plus adaptation (9)	NGO, university
	Hayes	Mitigation plus adaptation (9)	Environmentalist, NGO
	Worldwide Fund	Mitigation plus adaptation (9)	NGO
	Wisconsin Dept. Natural Resources	Mitigation plus adaptation (9)	Government
	Berger	Rights of nature (11)	Scientist
	Suzuki	Rights of nature (11)	Scientist, NGO
	Gore	Rights of nature (11)	Policymaker, government
	Scharper	Rights of nature (11)	Academic, university
	Friends of the Earth Int.	Rights of nature (11)	NGO
	Meyer-Abich	Rights of nature (11)	Academic

Evidence	Worldview	Proposed Actions
History, case studies	Moral, social construction	Work toward equality, continue to negotiate
Data	Social construction	Improve models
History, scientific lit, data	Social construction	Reduce emissions, prepare to adapt, work toward equality
Data, theory	Social construction	Work back from desirable scenarios
Anecdote, data	Nature robust	Do nothing
Data	Nature robust	Develop technology, build sustainability, do more research
Scientific lit	Nature robust	Do nothing
Data	Nature robust	Do nothing, improve models
Scientific lit	Nature robust	Do nothing
Scientific lit	Ecological	Reduce emissions, revise government incentives
Metaphor	Ecological	Restore people–nature balance
Theory	Ecological, religious	Build sustainability, work back from desirable scenarios
Policy	Ecological	No regrets
Case studies, expert testimony	Ecological	Do more research
Data	Ecological	Monitor, improve models
Data	Ecological	Build sustainability, do more research
Data, policy analysis	Ecological	Reduce emissions, restore people–nature balance
Theory	Religious	Reduce emissions, develop technology
Scientific lit, data, pictures	Nature fragile	Reduce emissions, back to nature, build sustainability
Data	Nature fragile	Reduce emissions, develop technology, revise government incentives
Scientific lit, data	Nature fragile	Reduce emissions, adopt Kyoto Protocol, prepare to adapt, educate, engage industry
Scientific lit, anecdote	Nature fragile	Reduce emissions, develop sinks
Scientific lit, metaphor	Nature fragile	Reduce emissions, revise government incentives
Scientific lit	Nature fragile	Reduce emissions, adopt Kyoto Protocol
History, anecdote	Ecological, nature fragile	Integrate climate change with other policy, restore people–nature balance
History, metaphor	Nature fragile, religious	Back to nature, restore people–nature balance
Scientific lit, anecdote	Nature fragile	Adopt Kyoto Protocol, work toward equality, reduce per capita emissions
Scientific lit, policy analysis	Nature fragile	Restore people–nature balance, educate, no regrets

UCINET Group	Author or Title	Argument Family (number)	Authority
	National Resources Defense Council	Rights of nature (11)	NGO
	Linden	Economics (8)	
	Burnett	Mitigation (6)	NGO
	Johansen	Mitigation (6)	Scientist and academic, NGO and university
	Chatterjee and Finger	Reduce inequality (10)	Academic, industry and university
	Gyawali	Reduce inequality (10)	Scientist, government
	McMichael	Reduce inequality (10)	Scientist, NGO
	Ahmed and Ahmed	Reduce inequality (10)	Environmentalist, NGO
	German Advisory Council on Global Change	Energy modernization (5)	NGO
2d	La Vina	Reduce inequality (10)	Environmentalist, NGO
	Athanasiou	Political modernization (4)	Environmentalist, NGO
3a	Benedick	Political modernization (4)	Policymaker, NGO
	IPCC WG2	Mitigation (6)	Scientists, NGO
3b	Goulder and Nadreau	Political modernization (4)	Academic, university
	Worldwatch Institute	Political modernization (4)	Environmentalist, NGO
	Ausubel Council for Ag	Could be good (2)	Academic, university
	Science and Technology	Could be good (2)	Scientist, NGO
	Califnornia National Assessment Report	Mitigation plus adaptation (9)	Scientist and academic, government and university
	Campaign for Nuclear Phaseout	Mitigation plus adaptation (9)	NGO
	Mid-Atlantic Regional Assessment	Mitigation plus adaptation (9)	Scientist, government
	Kirby	Energy modernization (5)	Environmentalist, research org
	Global Environmental Facility and UNDP	Energy modernization (5)	Government
	Porritt	Energy modernization (5)	Environmentalist, NGO
	US Energy Agency and AID	Energy modernization (5)	Policymaker and member of trade association, government and industry
	Lovins	Energy modernization (5)	Environmentalist, NGO
	US DOE Fossil Energy	Energy modernization (5)	Government
	Hoffert, Caldeira, Benford, et al.	Energy modernization (5)	Scientist, research org

Evidence	Worldview	Proposed Actions
Scientific lit, data	Nature fragile	Reduce emissions, continue to negotiate
Anecdote	Nature fragile	Engage industry
Scientific lit	Nature fragile	Educate, grow economies
Data	Nature fragile	Reduce emissions
History, scientific lit, expert testimony, policy analysis	Nature fragile	Integrate climate change into other policy, build sustainability, restore people–nature balance
Data, policy analysis	Nature fragile	Develop technology, monitor, do more research
Scientific lit, data	Nature fragile	Reduce emissions, control population, work toward equality
Data	Ecological, nature fragile	Integrate climate change with other policy, work toward equality
Scientific lit	Nature fragile	Reduce emissions, develop technology, build sustainability, fund projects, do more research
Data, policy analysis	Policy, nature fragile	Prepare to adapt, work toward equality, assist the most affected, educate
Scientific lit	Policy, nature fragile	Develop technology, integrate climate change with other policy
Anecdote, policy analysis	Modernization, policy	Develop technology, continue to negotiate
Scientific lit, data	Economic, modernization, policy	Develop technology, integrate climate change with other policy, build sustainability, do more research
Utilitarian, data	Modernization	Act–learn–act, continue to negotiate
History, data	Modernization	Reduce emissions, adopt Kyoto Protocol
Anecdote, data	Modernization	Develop technology, fund projects
Scientific lit, case studies	Modernization	Prepare to adapt, build sustainability, do more research
Case studies, anecdote	Modernization	Prepare to adapt, build sustainability, no regrets
Scientific lit, data	Modernization	Reduce emissions
Data	Modernization	Integrate climate change with other policy, educate, revise government incentives, improve models
Data, pictures	Modernization	Develop technology
Case studies, data	Modernization	Reduce emissions, develop technology
Data	Modernization	Reduce emissions, adopt Kyoto Protocol
Data	Modernization	Educate, no regrets
Data, theory	Modernization	Develop technology
Scientific lit, policy analysis	Modernization	Develop technology
Scientific lit, data	Modernization	Develop technology, do more research, continue to negotiate

UCINET Group	Author or Title	Argument Family (number)	Authority
	Inovest	Economics (8)	Member of trade org, industry
	Shackleton	Economics (8)	Scientist, government
	Browne	Mitigation (6)	Industry
	Minnesotans for an Energy-Efficient Economy	Mitigation (6)	NGO
	Hansen, Sato, Ruedy, Lacis and Oinas	Mitigation (6)	Scientist, research org
	IPCC WG3	Adaptation (7)	Scientist, NGO
	Stakhiv and Schilling	Adaptation (7)	Scientist, government
	UK Climate Impacts Programme	Adaptation (7)	Scientist, government
	Cohen	Science solutions (3)	Scientist, government
	Parks	Science solutions (3)	
	Huq	Reduce inequality (10)	Scientist, NGO
	Unfair Burden?	Reduce inequality (10)	Policymaker, government
	Greenwald, Roberts and Reomer	Reduce inequality (10)	Environmentalist, NGO
	Adhikary	Rights of nature (11)	NGO
3c	Koteen, Bloomfield, Eichler et al	Mitigation plus adaptation (9)	Environmentalist, research org, NGO
4	Meyerson	Mitigation (6)	Scientist
	Sathaye and Ravindranath	Mitigation (6)	Scientist, research org
	Ecimovic, Stuhler, Vezjak and Mulej	Science solutions (3)	Scientist, university
	Rosenzweig and Hillel	Adaptation (7)	Scientist, government

Evidence	Worldview	Proposed Actions
Data, policy analysis	Modernization	Emissions trading, do more research, revise government incentives
Scientific lit	Modernization	Work toward equality, no regrets
Case studies, data, metaphor	Modernization	Reduce emissions, build sustainability, no regrets, do more research
Case studies, data	Modernization	Reduce emissions, no regrets
Scientific lit, data	Modernization	Reduce emissions, develop technology
Scientific lit, data	Modernization	Prepare to adapt, monitor, do more research, improve models
Scientific lit	Modernization	Develop technology, integrate climate change with other policy
Policy analysis	Modernization	No regrets, act–learn–act
Scientific lit	Modernization	Educate, monitor, no regrets
Expert testimony	Modernization	Monitor, do more research
Policy analysis	Modernization	Prepare to adapt, continue to negotiate
Rights	Modernization	Developed countries first, integrate climate change with other policy
Case studies	Modernization	Assist most affected
Data, expert testimony	Modernization	Fund projects
Scientific lit, pictures	Modernization, ecological	Reduce emissions, prepare to adapt
Data	Modernization, nature fragile	Control population, reduce per capita emissions
Scientific lit, data	Modernization, nature fragile	No regrets
Data	Modernization, nature fragile	Build sustainability, continue to negotiate
Data	Modernization, nature fragile	Prepare to adapt, act–learn–act

8

Prospects for the Debate: Endless Recycling of Arguments or Movement towards Agreement?

Even at the relatively heady time surrounding the Rio environmental agreements in 1992, dissident voices could be heard. Indeed all the arguments that have both promoted and retarded 'coming to agreement' were present at that time: arguments about the science and the seriousness of climate change, who is to blame and who should pay for mitigation and adaptation, domination and inequality, and the deep distrust of modernity and modern solutions as opposed to rethinking human relationships with nature.

However, since the UNFCCC was ratified, the debate has not remained static. Scientific advances in understanding and monitoring the climate, better understanding of international processes (and more experience with them, for example in the World Trade Commission), the proliferation of NGOs with expertise in climate change issues, the continuing negotiations under the UNFCCC, and more reporting of alarming changes such as melting of glaciers and sea ice have all contributed to the evolution of the debate. Such evolutionary change has not been fast enough to satisfy people who fear the collapse of the climate system, nor slow enough to satisfy those who fear taking on a burden of costs when both problem and solutions remain highly uncertain.

If one element of the debate has received more emphasis than others, it is the scientific evidence. What is the nature of the evidence? Those looking for direct experience of 'global warming' have been pulled up short again and again. The excessively hot summer of 1988 seemed likely enough evidence that climate change was manifesting itself – likely enough to spark urgent calls for action from the US Congress. National Aeronautics and Space Administration scientist Jim Hansen testified before Congress that he was almost certain that hot weather was part of a pattern of human-induced climate change. But it was easy for people, including governmental policymakers, to retreat from such calls for action when temperatures returned to more normal ranges – and perhaps to feel that scientists had 'cried wolf'. Subsequent evidence about longer term warming trends has not generated enough support to establish widespread programmes to reduce greenhouse gas emissions, either in highly industrialized or non-industrialized countries. The empirical evidence as manifested in charts such as the one in the figure called the 'Keeling curve', which appears in Chapter 2, generally is not as convincing as people's experience of seasonal weather.

Seasonal weather changes are now emerging in a crescendo of reports, from melting ice to persistent droughts, from precipitation changes to pests that proliferate under warmer conditions, from bleached coral reefs to severe heat waves. However, for each report like this there are cautions about whether individual phenomena are signs of climate change (a long-term problem) or climate variability, pollution, over-exploitation of natural resources, over-development by humans, some other cause, or perhaps a combination of causes.

If the evidence itself seems indirect, the methodologies used to gather and interpret data on current conditions, and to model future climatic changes are highly techno-scientific, difficult to explain to non-scientists and easy to criticize. The 'greenhouse effect' itself is generally not well understood. Ways to measure the concentration of greenhouse gases and even to determine air temperature involve complex instrumentation, estimation and modelling (Norton and Suppe, 2001). Models of climate are routinely criticized for not including important variables, lacking the basis for verification and needing large-scale tuning factors (for example 'flux correction'). Scientific uncertainties are debated and acknowledged by scientists. For non-scientists to swallow the climate change hypothesis requires a generous helping of faith.

No wonder, then, despite increasing acceptance that climate change is occurring, that there is still lively discussion at the first and second stases[1] of the argument: What is happening and is this a problem?

The primacy of the scientific arguments cannot be ignored by those who frame climate change as a *social* problem – of economics, governance, human and nature relationships, or technology. These various social problems may exist, but if they are not manifested in resulting problems – such as 'killer smog' or nuclear 'accidents' – the fact that we construct them as problems is not in itself a reason to try to solve them, except, perhaps, theoretically or as part of our university humanities classes.

But there is no straight-line process from scientifically accepted evidence to widespread change in policies and behaviours. The need for scientific evidence and hypotheses to enter the realms of economics, politics and what has been called the public sphere make it at least advantageous and probably necessary to analyse the debate as a debate where science is an important contributor but by no means the only or most decisive one.

Thus I repeat that all arguments should be considered together. Because both the scientific construction of climate change and the relationship issues that are tied inextricably to climate change are essentially social in nature, these kinds of arguments can be examined on a more-or-less equal footing.

Instead of taking the scientific arguments as logically first or as more important in the debate – in other words saying that the prospect of climate change must be proven before we can talk about how to address the issue – arguments at all stases may be examined together.

Often this is how individuals, families, businesses, governments and other human groups solve problems through debate. People argue about causes at the same time they argue about tactics and solutions. Declines in sales for Company X's product may have one of several causes, but those who propose product improvements may make their arguments without regard to any cause. Legislators may not agree that a specific problem is serious, but they may pass a law anyway for any number of reasons. A family may agree on a course of action that none of them really likes simply because they agree that the family should be unified on the issue. Argumentation scholars may carefully separate the stases from one another and order them, but those of us who argue don't often fit the pattern or the ordering.

At this point it's worth recapping the investigation recorded in this book. In this study I have examined scientific and other types of arguments together. The debate as a whole must take cognizance of all arguments that have found at least partial adherence. And no type of argument can be ignored. The common assumption that we are waiting for scientists to tell us what to do is, on the one hand, not how things work in the world and, on the other hand, a delaying tactic with considerable downside potential. Scientists have pertinent information, to be sure – but so do those whose care it is to provide food, shelter, healthcare, and a host of other goods and services for people. None of the participants in the debate holds the pure truth, but each holds a few threads woven into the fabric of human life here and now.

Partial Views

Given the messiness of debate and of problem-solving in general, we should not be surprised when approaches that appear to be helpful often are not. Four examples offer some insights into areas of the debate but finally fail to address all arguments on their own terms. Rather, each considers one perspective as the most important and downplays others.

Example 1: The Political View

As a power struggle, the process of addressing climate change at a global scale provides rich fodder for political scientists and analysts, especially those who study social movements and protests. Research on the political opportunities and resources available to non-governmental groups focuses on political power and special interests. International relations analysts examine how countries agree (or disagree) on the terms of environmental agreements. However, two assumptions pervade most of these analyses. One is that power and politics are at the base of all the arguments; the second is that everyone in the political debate is simply trying to maximize his or her own gains. But many arguments are explicitly *not* political, but instead concern identity and solidarity (perhaps through shared interests, or through shared kinship, ethnicity, experiences and other elements), economic and cultural activities, and so on. Self-interest is not necessarily the most important element in a debate – or even in choosing to act. Many of the arguments in the climate change debate appeal to idealism, or to self-interest in the long term of future generations. So analyses that start by assuming that everything's political do not serve the analysis of the climate change debate well.

Example 2: The Cultural View

Cultural arguments examine how climate change is framed according to cultural worldviews and about how debaters attempt to have people identify themselves as, for example, 'global citizens'. That is, how a person thinks about social solidarity and about his or her place in society will determine both the framing of climate change as a problem (or non-problem) and the acceptable solutions. These are useful concepts and constructs (and will be discussed again later in this chapter). But, again, this is a partial vision of the debate, since it neglects politics, scientific evidence and economics.

Example 3: The Scientific View

Focusing on science and scientists yields another set of partial insights into the climate change debate. The examination of how scientists make truth and build scientific consensus is an invaluable element in areas of the debate that are about or rest on scientific evidence. The most important result from research into the workings of science is that, although science is indeed a particular brand of truth-making, with its own rules-of-the-game, scientists have no very special claim to ultimate truths that must be accepted unquestioningly by non-scientists. This result from sociologists of science creates the level playing field within which all arguments, both scientific and non-scientific, can be examined together. However, these tools are usually used to deconstruct scientific claims – that is to strip science of its 'objective' mystique and show that it works like other social processes – more than to discern bases for agreement among scientists and other groups. Typically, scientific discourse is exposed as metaphorical, rhetorical, political or narrative instead of objective and rational. However, as Richard Brown and I have noted (Brown and Malone, 2004, p120):

> *Science persistently refuses to collapse into politics ... far from exposing science as just another ideological or marketing fraud, this understanding prompts us to protect and nurture ethical dispassion, acceptance of criticism, tolerance for dissent, and appeals to reason and evidence that are built and sustained by the norms and ideals of scientific communities.*

Scientific arguments have certain claims to truth that should be recognized, just as other arguments have other types of claims to other truths.

Example 4: The Environmental Sociological View

Environmental sociology would seem to have direct relevance to global climate change issues and the debate, but environmental sociologists have paid very little explicit attention to arguments made about global environmental changes. Instead, they focus on issues of the relationship between human beings and nature. They *make* arguments but do not examine the debate. Those who identify themselves as environmental sociologists in the US have tackled such issues as providing an alternative view to the classical sociological assumption that human beings are superior to and can manage nature. European theorists such as Ulrich Beck have adopted a critical theory stance, providing sharply detailed analyses of where modernity has gone wrong *vis-à-vis* the environment. Again, the questions of the right relationship with nature and the role of world inequalities (including colonialism) in damaging the environment are threads in the fabric of the debate, but by no means the whole debate. The climate change debate includes speakers and writers who believe that modern management of nature is necessary and desirable as well as those who believe that human beings should get out of the nature-management business. Both views must be examined together, without judging which is better or which could 'win'.

Searching for Wider Views

The difference in foci of these analyses illustrates a difficulty in analysing the debate. An assumption that, at bottom, the debate is really about one thing – about, say, politically oriented rational action, or about whose knowledge is legitimate, or about the human–nature relationship – precludes an ability to see the debate whole, with its varying motivations, goals and strategies.

I turned from these partial insights to globalization theorists, reasoning that globalization is by definition a multidisciplinary topic. Globalization issues in many respects parallel those of climate change: both include economic, political and cultural dimensions of a world becoming both more the same and more different. Globalization theorists include topic areas that are, for many debaters about climate change, at the heart of the issue: inequality, development, and the relationship of nations to one another and to the non-human environment. Global science and global environmental pollution and change are included in the purview of some globalization theorists as well.

The classification of both globalization and climate change theories and arguments into political, economic and cultural emphases provided an initial mapping of the dimensions in the debate. Speakers/writers indeed argue from particular worldviews that reduce the issues to one dimension and then translate other messages into the language of that dimension. A good example is an economic argument that discusses cultural (in other words non-priced) aspects of the climate change debate in economic terms, thus creating such problematic notions as a 'willingness-to-pay' for protected environments and the 'existence value' of, for example, iconic locations (Mount Fuji, the Grand Canyon, and so on). Attempts to price the environment and to create, for example, water markets, have had only limited success. Indeed, it appears that many parks and wonders of the natural world are not very highly valued in monetary terms – although most people do indeed favour having parks and preserving natural beauties.

If the comparison with globalization theory illuminates a principal aspect of both debates – the tendency to reduce everything to a common approach or metric – it also neglects another principal element of the climate change debate – the role of science. Globalization theorists tend to black-box science as an enabler of globalization (in modern transport and communication, for instance) or as one part of a culture whose more interesting aspects are the arts, fashion, the way folk practices and arts become consumer products or museum artefacts, and so on.

The Argument Analysis

From these more theoretical musings, I turned to an empirical study for the necessary complement, correction and spur to creating better theoretical constructs. A direct examination of actual arguments made in the climate change debate may validate, undermine or extend one or more of the theories reviewed and provide new ways of thinking about this debate and perhaps about other debates. For example, if I could extend the categorization matrix of climate change theories developed in the discussion of globalization and use framing analysis (Goffman, 1974), I could perhaps show how arguments in one domain can be reframed around similarities in rhetorical elements – a complex effort but, if achievable, one that would build theory and provide practical help to debaters wishing to come to agreement.

The 100 documents examined for this study represent a wide range of the argument space in the climate change debate[2] (although not, as noted in Chapter 5, a representation of the *shares* of each argument in that space). Using the objective classification scheme provided by classical and modern theorists of rhetoric and argumentation provided a framework that is not anchored in a single dimension (political, economic, cultural, scientific) of the debate. Nor does a rhetorical analysis put any special emphasis (positive or negative) on scientific arguments *vis-à-vis* other types of arguments. Thus, arguments are seen *as arguments*, and the focus is kept on the wide debate space.

To conduct a comparative analysis of the arguments, I identified the coherent arguments themselves and four principal rhetorical features of each argument: the authority of the speaker/writer (as given by his or her professional position and affiliation), the type(s) of evidence used to support the claims made, the worldview(s) expressed and the action(s) proposed. Using this framework allowed both comparison of the arguments and clustering of them into 'families' of coherent arguments, ranging from denials of the hypotheses that the climate is changing and that people are contributing to the changes, to impassioned advocacy for making immediate changes in human activities to mitigate effects on the world's climate.

Families cohere not only around statements of the arguments but also in terms of sources of authority, types of evidence and worldview – especially worldview. The comparative analysis shows that different worldviews are strongly associated with families. The families also exhibit some basic agreements and numerous affiliations *across* families. Basic agreements include the following:

- All families take the question of climate change seriously, and none rules the prospect out completely. Even the sceptics treat the hypothesis as unproven rather than as false; most agree that there is evidence that atmospheric concentrations of carbon dioxide are rising, for example, although they dispute the meaning of the evidence.
- All agree that vast uncertainties exist, although again the implications of uncertainties are disputed. Some claim that uncertainty is a reason to wait and see, or to do further research and monitoring. Others view uncertainty as a reason to address the potential for climate change swiftly and effectively.
- All agree that climate change involves issues of societal wellbeing and lifestyle. Increased greenhouse gas emissions are principally the products of industrialization and modern farming methods, and of rising demands for food and goods by an increasing global population. Proposals for reducing emissions of greenhouse gases and adapting to climate change impacts such as sea-level rise raise issues of societal development, inequality, the relationship between human beings and the rest of nature, and the credibility of science in providing evidence of a problem and pathways towards solutions.
- All argue from definition, although some families also include cause-and-effect arguments. That is, the rhetorical basis of the arguments concerns the definition of the issue as a scientific or political one, whether or not the evidence can be defined as climate change, whether or not climate change can be defined as problematic, whether climate change is a technical problem solvable by new technology or a systemic problem solvable only by a retreat from technology, and so on.
- Families share a commitment to science. There are scientists in every family, and scientists are the most prominent debaters in eight of 11 families.
- Similarly, at least some members of all families use scientific literature and data as evidence for their argumentative claims. The predominant types of evidence used by all families except #10 and #11 are data and scientific literature.

These basic agreements at least keep members of different families talking to one another, although they may not provide enough of a foundation to come to agreement.

The social network analysis also explored common rhetorical elements across family lines – members of different families who have the same claims to authority or use the same kinds of evidence or hold the same worldview or advance the same proposals for action.

The social network analysis explored these cross-family links, positing that any of the rhetorical elements of their arguments constituted network ties among speakers/writers. If families hold strong ties in common, with few links across families, there would be little basis for thinking that the overall debate contained pathways for coming to agreement. That is, if all coherent arguments are closed off from other arguments, groups in the debate are simply talking to themselves without the possibility of building agreement.

I analysed the elements together to get a sense of whether family members are just talking to each other and are cut off from other families, or whether members have significant connections outside their own families. The results showed a dense network of ties, with the strongest correlation between worldview and overall linkages. The bases for coming to agreement as demonstrated by network ties include the following:

- Although the most common links are by worldview, these links are by no means purely identified with families. Even the members of Families #1 and #2 ('No problem!' and 'Climate Change Could Be Good for You') span four different worldviews, and the members in Families #4–9, who agree that 'More Modernization Is the Answer', hold eight of the nine worldviews (all but the view that nature is robust and will survive anything human beings could do).
- Similarly, links by worldview is a poor predictor of other links, which prove to be diverse. People can hold a basic worldview in common and yet both disagree among themselves and agree with people who hold other worldviews about what argument to make, evidence to use and actions to advocate. The nine members of one sub-network all espouse an economic worldview, but the group contains only five scientists, seven speakers/writers from NGOs,[3] five arguments using data as evidence and four proposals to develop new technologies. Another sub-network, whose 11 members hold the worldview that nature is socially constructed, are almost all scientists or academics and predominantly (seven members) at universities – but they differ in family membership (five families), type of evidence used (eight types) and actions proposed (18 different actions).
- Looking at the ties other than worldview also indicates potential bases for coming to agreement. For example, if debaters can agree on one or more actions they wish to see taken, they may be able to put aside (or at least table) other differences among them. For example, the recommendation to

develop new technologies to address climate change is made by 21 speakers/writers in eight of eleven families, spanning six of the nine worldviews.

- Although speakers/writers tend to have close ties to other members of their families, they also frequently have multiple ties outside their families – to fellow members of a profession or employees of the same type of organization, a preference for certain types of evidence, a worldview, and/or proposed actions. Any of these ties can link individuals and families, providing a basis for agreement on at least one aspect of the climate change issue.

Potential Pathways to Agreement

If there are *bases* for agreement, why do people persist in disagreeing? With this question we come back to theories of how people debate, change, come to some level of agreement, act to change a situation, then debate again. In Chapter 4 we approached this theoretical discussion by examining ideas about the ideal speech act and the orientation of speakers towards coming to agreement. But this is only one voice in a conversation about how people come to agree.

Another view involves the idea of a co-evolution of modern functional systems, such as the political, economic and scientific systems (see, for example, Luhmann, 1984). In previous eras, these systems were integrated, but with time they have come to be separate spheres of action. People act within one or another of them and emphasize the differences among them, as well as their relative importance. Hence, as in the earlier chapter's discussion of globalization, it is possible to look at an issue as a purely economic or purely political or purely social or purely some other system issue.

However, the complexity of modern functional systems and subsystems means that any attempt at intervention, any management plan, becomes one impulse among many, with effects that may or may not be intended but which are impossible to foresee because the integrative vision has been lost. Communication between or among systems has become highly unlikely.

This line of reasoning seems to lead to despair – a post-modern landscape of lonely individuals unable to communicate with one another. But, against this vision, things *do* change, and sometimes for the better. In the area of the environment, the world has become more aware of environmental issues and environmental protection laws do exist and are (at least partly) enforced (Weingart, 1990). Therefore, we should focus our attention on *how* it happens that people communicate effectively and agree on a course of action.

Another view of how people come to agree is that, as a response to the excesses of modernity, people are rediscovering their connections with the natural world. There are both historical and future-oriented explanations for this shift. Looking back, people realize that modern life is too detached from human roots in nature and that people need to return to the pre-modern direct human–nature relationship of mutual dependence. When human beings respect the rights of other elements of nature to exist in a state of wellbeing, they will not degrade the environment. Looking forward, people, when they are advanced materially, develop 'post-material values' that include environmental ethics, as Ronald Inglehart says (Inglehart, 1977 and 1990). As this ethical shift proceeds, people will increasingly agree that the human species is grounded in its environment and that its environment must be accounted for. Having agreed on post-material values, people may then agree on actions to understand and live in harmony with the rest of nature.

Another view comes from political realists and neo-realists, who frame the issue of coming to agreement as a matter of competing interests among countries as actors which are only concerned with their positions in the world relative to other countries and to their own wellbeing. Thus, the desire of each country for power, coupled with a recognition of limits to power (transaction costs), will drive countries to agree about matters that tend towards their mutual benefit, such as protecting resources that are available to all – the global commons, including the oceans, atmosphere and climate. Or nations may severally attempt to free-ride, in other words not pay the costs of protecting environmental resources but enjoy the benefits of others doing so. In either case, countries are the principal actors, and environmental agreements depend upon country-level leadership and actions.

Other political theorists hold that new ways of dealing with the environment – new international institutions – will arise as evidence emerges that there are needs to address, such as pollution, over-fishing and other issues, including climate change. These institutions will provide the impetus to action and the persistence to eventually effect change. However, these international regimes must ultimately work through governments, and governments may successfully resist if they feel their interests are threatened (Haas et al, 1993).

But institutions do change, whether or not countries change. One of the best known concepts used to describe the broader process of institutional change that is not limited to states is epistemic communities. The term was first coined in the 1970s and came to prominence in the 1990s to describe an alternative approach to studying international policy.[4] An epistemic community is 'a network of professionals with recognized expertise and competence in a particular domain or issue-area' (Haas, 1992, p3). Such a network has (a) shared values and principles, (b) shared beliefs about what causes the problems they are concerned with, (c) shared ideas about what is valid, and (d) a common policy enterprise. (This list sounds like the elements of an argument, doesn't it?) The epistemic community concept thus joins knowledge and power – in other words, scientists and policymakers; it is typically international and includes people within and outside of governmental structures.

What do economists have to say about coming to agreement? There are agreements to buy and sell, of course. How people decide to spend money or invest in public goods depends upon their perceptions of their needs, problems to be addressed and risks involved in various choices. Although economic theory posits people as acting out of private self-interest, society as a whole acts according to utilitarian principles, that is, to provide the greatest good for the greatest number. This is not the same as the sum total of individual maximizing actions (Arrow, 1951). Because markets are not perfect and economists have proved that general wellbeing could not result from the sum of self-interested actions, management of the economy is seen to be necessary, although how this should be accomplished in specific cases is itself a matter for discussion and debate. Coming to agreement is typically based on a demonstration that the costs of addressing climate change will be small, and wellbeing (or at least avoidance of damages) will be worth the costs.

These theories emphasize different aspects of the rhetorical elements that I have analysed as ties among related arguments and elements of the arguments. The theory that self-interest dominates the possibility for agreement – and maybe negates any such possibility – derives from a denial that any social network ties exist among people as individuals, societies or countries. But this is patently false. Even those seeking wealth and power at the expense of others presume the social relationships that will allow them to accumulate and that will validate the status of wealth and power. (What is the use of either if others do not acknowledge them?) And most of us value our family and social relationships as much as or more than wealth and power.

Theories about how institutions evolve and realign into new regimes and about epistemic communities involve analyses of ties formed by personal association (position and organization), the subject matter of the issue (like the argument families), the evidence, worldview, and proposed solutions. Without these elements, institutional regimes would fragment into impotency (as sometimes happens) and epistemic communities would not form.

In the end, there are as many theories about how people come to agreement as there are about how society is structured and changes. This is because arguing or debating – that is, language – is a principal non-violent medium through which people understand themselves as social beings and negotiate their daily and longer-term interactions. Language, used in argumentative debates, is the common medium for the processes described by theorists of all stripes. These theorists describe many particular mechanisms by which language works to build or maintain social solidarity and allot varying importance to them.

The various phases and places of the climate change debate have also received more or less emphasis. Some feel that individual worldviews and convictions – a form of almost religious belief – is the right focus for the debate; out of individual identities that rest on environmental values will emerge needed societal actions. Others stress the need for community-based debate and action. Yet another group examines the relationship between scientists and non-scientists, and identifies 'boundary objects' – images and concepts – that will allow effective communication to take place (Star and Griesemer, 1989). Still others feel that international agreements that prescribe actions are the critical factor in the debate.

But the common element here is language (talk, argument, conversation, debate). Social systems, post-material values, new institutions, epistemic communities, cosmopolitan public spheres, a discourse of mobilization, boundary objects, framings – all conceptualize spaces and mechanisms for communication, argumentation and coming to agreement.

The presence of many forms of talk demonstrates the vibrancy of the debate, as Chapter 5 also showed. If some are exasperated at the competing arguments and ideas, the plus side is that societies are generating many ideas and experiments in greenhouse gas mitigation and now, increasingly, in adaptation. Since climate change is a complex problem with many implications for lifestyle and societal development, a plethora of viewpoints and ingenuities is very much needed.

But it is not chaos. The social world is not a mush of free-floating arguments, a post-modern sea of equal-meaning rhetorical statements. Neither is the social world rigidly and almost solely determined by the privileged knowledge of elite policymakers, corporate boards and scientists. Some arguments persuade more than others; some logically unassailable arguments are never taken up by those who could act in response to them. That is to say, the social world cannot be predicted exclusively by structure, nor by functional relationships, nor by random movements. The ideal speech act, systems theory, epistemic communities, and other frameworks and tools fall short of providing full explanation, much less predictive capability.

In Chapter 1, I talked about a spectrum of possible responses that individuals, groups and societies might have when confronted with new types of problems. At one end of this spectrum, people turn their heads or say 'No!' and do nothing. At the other end, they turn with passion to address or fight the problem in every way they can think of. Between the ends of this spectrum, individuals and groups and societies debate the issue and any side issues that might arise, trying to assess the problem, the seriousness of the problem, possible actions and everything else.

But in all these responses, individuals, groups and societies attempt, first, to connect new problems with their experience and, second, to develop solidarities based on shared trust and knowledge. Again, a principal medium of these attempts is language. In discourse, in arguments, they make connections based on shared understandings, attempt to co-create further shared understandings and work towards increasing their audiences' adherence to certain arguments.

Thus the climate change issue has been fitted into many frames, as shown in the arguments and argument families. In presenting an argument, a debater puts that argument into a frame that he or she thinks will be acceptable to the audience. Members of that audience may then make sense of the argument in the way the speaker wants them to. If, for example, the 'Man versus Nature' argument makes sense to an audience – that human beings have to struggle and control nature – an interpretation made by a speaker that climate change can be fitted to this frame will probably make sense to that audience. Economics, politics, culture and science provide at least partial framings for arguments in the climate change debate space. But these framings are being continually reconstructed and re-imagined as new information enters the debate – new participants, new organizations, new evidence, new worldviews or new statements of worldviews, and new proposals. Debaters consciously react to others in the conversation, moving closer to or further away from agreement. Stable images, like the 'big blue marble' or the greenhouse, may have multiple meanings, and users of those images select meanings that they feel will increase the adherence of their audiences to the argument presented.

Several widely shared bases for agreement emerge from this analysis. First, the middle argument families ('More Modernization', Families #4–9) all affirm that people can manage nature: extract resources, develop technologies, and exploit intangibles such as scenery and space. (The ability to manage nature can also be defined by its double: the ability or choice *not* to manage nature.) Scientists, technology developers and others may make mistakes that result in undesirable outcomes (pollution, disease and so on), but these can be corrected through better technologies and institutional arrangements.

Most of the proposals about climate change mitigation and adaptation rest on this underlying belief and, thus, it provides a widely shared basis for agreement. By a process of association (Perelmen and Olbrechts-Tyteca, 1969), speakers and writers characterize climate change as the same class of problem as many success stories: the ban on DDT (and development of other pesticides), Superfund-type cleanups, the agreement to eliminate ozone-depleting substances, even the race to the moon and the Manhattan Project. Similarly, associating climate change with another kind of success story, speakers/writers may invoke the history of energy technology development, citing the need to transform the energy system to one that is environmentally benign. First there was small-scale biomass burning, then coal, then oil, then nuclear fission (with solar and hydropower becoming more used as technologies improve). The next transition may be simply another transformation, but this time mindfully harmless to the environment.

Second, the predominance of scientific voices in the debate provides a thing-in-common. The history and achievements of science and technology provide the basis for devising science-and-technology-based strategies to address climate change. But, by the same token, the existence of scientific disciplines and professional specialties ensures that there will be plenty of disagreement about what actions to take and the priorities of any set of actions. These can be couched as disagreements or differences in orientation – in other words whether it is more important to get political and policy agreements in place, get the economic markets right, jump-start new technologies and promote technology transfer, or change people's consumption expectations and habits. Or more specific disagreements emerge: nuclear versus renewable energy, energy conservation/efficiency versus big technology, mitigation versus adaptation.

And third, about half of the 100 documents use data and models as evidence to back their arguments. This reflects the predominance of scientists in the debate but also links scientists to policymakers and NGO participants, for whom facts, data and models provide valuable support for more explicitly value-based arguments. Such arguments contain much common ground and many potential bases for agreement. Moreover, these arguments continue to be cognizant of other arguments – for example, acknowledgements of great uncertainties and advocacy of 'no regrets' actions, which can also appeal to those who think Nature is fragile and advocate the precautionary principle. The lively debate continues about global climate change, leading to the expertise and institutional capabilities that have resulted in an increasing orientation towards coming to agreement and an increase in links among debate participants that can provide bases for agreement.

But agreement is never total, always partial – open to multiple rounds of reinterpretation and compromise. The UNFCCC provides a great deal of strategic ambiguity because different Parties to the Convention needed to be able to interpret its provisions in different ways. To succeed, subsequent agreements must allow for diversity in situations and capabilities. That is, they must allow for diverse connections among people, leading to accommodation of multiple authorities, arguments, evidence, worldviews and actions.

Moving towards agreement out of a sea of partial agreements, disagreements and changing knowledge needs to be based on an understanding of the potential for agreement.

One fruitless approach is holding out for an ideal pathway forward, where everyone agrees about everything from the definition of the climate change issue to the steps to address it. Everyone's cultural understandings and lifestyles (or lifestyle aspirations) are involved in the energy, agricultural and industrial systems that are contributing to climate change. This complex situation guarantees that a united understanding and agreement on action is an impossible dream.

The extension of not waiting for universal agreement is the recognition that we will argue about various aspects of climate change (meaning, impacts, actions) *at the same time* that we undertake actions. These actions will be necessarily experimental and partial; the successful ones will need to be scaled up (another issue to debate). And different societies will be doing very different things. Coastal communities, for instance, will try to understand and adapt to sea-level rise and, if they think them likely, more severe storms. Probably decreasing greenhouse gas emissions will be a second priority. For a host of reasons, including climate change, industries might embark on innovation projects that are both unprecedented and profitable. And so on.

And there's little use in waiting for the one – or even the set of – solutions that will solve the problem. This is perhaps as much or more of a mirage than striving for full, unified, end-to-end understanding. I'm tempted to characterize such a solution or solution set as a construct that will be satisfactory to no one. Any action that has a hope of being agreed to and implemented will be what a group of social scientists has called 'clumsy' solutions – actions that 'creatively combine all opposing perspectives on what the problems are and how they should be resolved' (Verweij et al, 2006). These scientists were talking specifically about clumsy policies, but the principle applies to any complex problem (in other words one that affects many societies and social systems) and any proposed solutions.

This is where the good news about social network ties provides a crucial insight into the development and implementation of proposed actions that can be agreed on and implemented. Pragmatically, such proposals have to offer something to most or all of their stakeholders – but the 'somethings' may range from professional or organizational solidarity to satisfactory evidence to provisions that accommodate various worldviews to simple agreement on the action (for whatever reasons).

Another insight from social network analysis is that, paradoxically, we can look for agreement both where substantial agreement exists already and where diversity exists. Where those in the climate change debate share many links, they can build on their shared links. Where more diversity exists, debaters need to be more thoughtful about seeking common ground, looking at a range of elements that might be agreed on. Furthermore, having many elements in the mix allows multiple fallback or compromise positions to emerge. The strategically ambiguous concepts of cost–benefit analysis (where costs and benefits mean more than money) and sustainability can, for example, facilitate conceptual agreements that allow conversations to continue.

Notes

1 See Chapter 4 for a discussion of the stases.
2 See www.earthscan.co.uk/dcc for a first-stage analysis of each of the 100 arguments considered in this book.
3 Recall that some documents have multiple authors.
4 See Antoniades (2003) for a history of the phrase.

References

Antoniades, A. (2003) 'Epistemic communities, epistemes and the construction of (world) politics', *Global Society*, vol 17, pp21–38
Arrow, K. (1951) *Social Choice and Individual Values*, John Wiley, New York
Brown, R. H. and Malone, E. L. (2004) 'Reason, politics, and the politics of truth: How science is both autonomous and dependent', *Sociological Theory*, vol 22, pp106–122
Goffman, E. (1974) *Frame Analysis: An Essay on the Organization of Experience*, 1986 reprint, Harper and Row, New York
Haas, P. M. (1992) 'Knowledge, power and international policy coordination', *International Organization*, vol 46, p1
Haas, P. M., Keohane, R. O. and Levy, M. A. (eds) (1993) *Institutions for the Earth: Sources of Effective International Environmental Protection*, MIT Press, Cambridge, MA
Inglehart, R. (1977) *The Silent Revolution: Changing Values and Political Styles among Western Publics*, Princeton University Press, Princeton, NJ

Inglehart, R. (1990) *Culture Shift in Advanced Industrial Society*, Princeton University Press, Princeton, NJ

Luhmann, N. (1984) *Social Systems*, trans. J. Bednarz and D. Baecker, 1995 reprint, Stanford University Press, Stanford, CA

Norton, S. D. and Suppe, F. (2001) 'Why atmospheric modeling is good science', in C. A. Miller and P. N. Edwards (eds) *Changing the Atmosphere: Expert Knowledge and Environmental Governance*, MIT Press, Cambridge, MA

Perelmen, C. and Olbrechts-Tyteca, L. (1969) *The New Rhetoric: A Treatise on Argumentation*, trans. J. Wilkinson and P. Weaver, 1971 reprint, University of Notre Dame Press, Notre Dame, IN

Rayner, S. (1995) 'A contractual map of human values for climate change decision-making', in A. Katama (ed) *Equity and Social Considerations Related to Climate Change*, ICIPE Science Press, Nairobi

Star, S. L., and Griesemer, J. R. (1989) 'Institutional ecology, "translations" and boundary objects: Amateurs and professionals in Berkeley's Museum of Vertebrate Zoology, 1907–1939', *Social Studies of Science*, vol 19, pp387–420

Steger, M. A. E., Pierce, J. C., Steel, G. S. and Lovrich, N. P. (1989) 'Political culture, post-material values, and the new environmental paradigm: A comparative analysis of Canada and the United States', *Political Behavior*, vol 3, pp233–254

Thompson, M., Ellis, R. and Wildavsky, A. (1990) *Cultural Theory*, Westview, Boulder, CO

Thompson, M., Rayner, S., Gerlach, L. P., Grubb, M, Lach, D., Ney, S., Paterson, M., Rose, A. and Timmerman, P. (1998) 'Cultural discourses', in S. Rayner and E. L. Malone (eds) *Human Choice and Climate Change, Volume 1: The Societal Framework*, Battelle Press, Columbus, OH

Van Liere, K. D. and Dunlap, R. E. (1980) 'The social bases of environmental concern: A review of hypotheses, explanations and empirical evidence', *Public Opinion Quarterly*, vol 2, pp181–197

Verweij, M., Douglas, M., Ellis, R., Engel, C., Hendriks, F., Lohmann, S., Ney, S., Rayner, S. and Thompson, M. (2006) 'Clumsy solutions for a complex world: The case of climate change', *Public Administration*, vol 84, no 4, pp817–843

Weingart, P. (1990) 'Doomed to passivity? The global ecological crisis and the social sciences', in H. Krugg (ed) *Technikpolitik Angesichts der Umweltkatastrophe*, Physica-Verlag, Heidelberg, Germany

Appendix 1

Arguments Sorted by Family with Coded Rhetorical Features

See page 85 for code explanations. See www.earthscan.co.uk/dcc for a first-stage analysis of each of the 100 arguments.

DocNum	DocName	FAM	AU	OR	EV	WV	AC1	AC2	AC3	AC4	AC5	Y
#022	CALDER	FAM01	AUACA	ORUNI	EVSCT	WVROB	ACZER	0	0	0	0	Y1998
#030	SINGER	FAM01	AUSCI	ORUNI	EVDAT	WVROB	ACZER	ACMDL	0	0	0	Y2000
#046	LINDZE	FAM01	AUSCI	ORUNI	EVSCT	WVPLY	ACTEC	ACRCH	ACZER	0	0	Y2003
#003	AUSUBE	FAM02	AUACA	ORUNI	EVANE EVDAT	WVMOD	ACTEC	ACFND	0	0	0	Y2001
#023	IDSOCD	FAM02	0	ORNGO	EVSCT	WVROB	ACZER	0	0	0	0	Y2002
#034	APIPOS	FAM02	AUTRA	ORIND	EVDAT	WVECN	ACTEC	ACRCH	ACINC	0	0	Y1997
#059	CASTEC	FAM02	AUSCI	ORNGO	EVSCT EVCAS	WVMOD	ACADA	ACSUS	ACRCH	0	1	Y1992
#073	USDOST	FAM02	0	ORGOV	EVDAT	WVROB	ACTEC	ACSUS	ACRCH	0	1	Y2003
#074	COONCH	FAM02	AUACA	ORNGO	EVPAN	WVECN	ACTEC	ACRCH	0	0	0	Y2002
#081	GLOBAL	FAM02	AUTRA	ORIND	EVDAT	WVECN	ACTEC	ACZER	0	0	0	Y1997
#087	WHATAB	FAM02	0	ORNGO	EVANE EVDAT	WVROB	ACZER	0	0	0	0	0
#009	MARTEN	FAM03	AUSCI	ORRES	EVDAT	WVECO	ACSUS	ACRCH	0	0	1	Y1994
#019	DARWIN	FAM03	AUSCI	ORGOV	EVDAT	WVECO	ACMON	ACMDL	0	0	0	Y1996
#038	COHENS	FAM03	AUSCI	ORGOV	EVSCT	WVMOD	ACEDU	ACMON	ACNRG	0	0	Y1993
#039	ECIMOV	FAM03	AUSCI	ORUNI	EVDAT	WVMOD ACSUS WVNAT		ACNEG	0	0	1	Y2002
#041	VANASS	FAM03	AUSCI	ORRES	EVDAT	WVSCO	ACMDL	0	0	0	0	Y2002
#053	PARKSN	FAM03	0	0	EVEXP	WVMOD	ACMON	ACRCH	0	0	0	Y2002
#054	TAUBES	FAM03	0	ORRES	EVCAS EVEXP	WVECO	ACRCH	0	0	0	0	Y1997
#085	SLADEH	FAM03	AUPOL	ORGOV	EVHIS	WVPLY	ACINT	ACSUS	ACNRG	ACRCH	1	Y2000
#086	ASHFOR	FAM03	AUSCI	ORNGO	EVDAT	WVECN	ACEDU	ACMON	ACRCH	0	0	Y2001
#002	BENEDI	FAM04	AUPOL	ORNGO	EVANE EVPAN	WVMOD WVPLY	ACTEC	ACNEG	0	0	0	Y2001
#005	GOULDE	FAM04	AUACA	ORUNI	EVUTI EVDAT	WVMOD	ACALA	ACNEG	0	0	0	Y2002
#013	EDWARD	FAM04	AUSCI	ORUNI	EVHIS EVDAT	WVSCO	ACMDL	ACALA	0	0	0	Y1996
#020	ATHANA	FAM04	AUENV	ORNGO	EVSCT	WVPLY WVNAT	ACTEC	ACINT	0	0	0	Y2003
#060	SANDAL	FAM04	AUSCI	ORNGO ORUNI	EVSCT EVPAN	WVPLY WVSCO	ACKYO	0	0	0	0	Y2001
#075	ROBINS	FAM04	AUTRA	ORGOV	EVEXP	WVPLY	ACKYO	0	0	0	0	Y2002

DocNum	DocName	FAM	AU	OR	EV	WV	AC1	AC2	AC3	AC4	AC5	Y
#079	BLANCH	FAM04	0	ORNGO	EVRIT EVDAT	WVPLY	ACEMI	ACCNC	ACDIF	ACETR	0	Y2001
#097	WORLDW	FAM04	AUENV	ORNGO	EVHIS EVDAT	WVMOD	ACEMI	ACKYO	0	0	0	Y2002
#010	USEAUS	FAM05	AUPOL AUTRA	ORGOV ORIND	EVDAT	WVMOD	ACEDU	ACNRG	0	0	0	Y1999
#024	HOFFER	FAM05	AUSCI	ORRES	EVSCT EVDAT	WVMOD	ACTEC	ACRCH	ACNEG	0	0	Y2002
#026	KAWASH	FAM05	AUSCI	ORGOV	EVPAN	WVECO	ACNRG	0	0	0	0	Y2000
#065	PORRIT	FAM05	AUENV AUSCI	ORNGO	EVDAT	WVMOD	ACEMI	ACKYO	0	0	0	Y2003
#068	WORLDE	FAM05	AUENV	ORNGO	EVPAN	WVPLY WVECN	ACEMI	ACTEC	ACETR	ACEQU	ACSUS	Y1998
#082	GEFUND	FAM05	0	ORGOV	EVCAS EVDAT	WVMOD	ACEMI	ACTEC	0	0	0	0
#089	KIRBYA	FAM05	AUENV	ORRES	EVDAT EVPIX	WVMOD	ACTEC	0	0	0	0	Y1999
#095	GERMAN	FAM05	0	ORNGO	EVSCT	WVNAT	ACEMI	ACTEC	ACSUS	ACFND	ACRCH	Y2003
#096	DOEFEN	FAM05	0	ORGOV	EVSCT EVPAN	WVMOD	ACTEC	0	0	0	0	Y1999
#100	AMORYL	FAM05	AUENV	ORNGO	EVDAT EVTHE	WVMOD	ACTEC	0	0	0	0	Y1999
#007	MEYERS	FAM06	AUSCI	0	EVDAT	WVMOD WVNAT	ACPOP	ACPCE	0	0	0	Y2002
#040	SATHAY	FAM06	AUSCI	ORRES	EVSCT EVDAT	WVMOD WVNAT	ACNRG	0	0	0	0	Y1998
#047	BROWNE	FAM06	AUTRA	ORIND	EVCAS EVDAT EVMET	WVMOD	ACEMI	ACSUS	ACNRG	ACRCH	1	Y1997
#049	IPCTWO	FAM06	AUSCI	ORNGO	EVSCT EVDAT	WVECN WVMOD WVPLY	ACTEC	ACINT	ACSUS	ACRCH	1	Y2001
#069	BURNET	FAM06	AUSCI	ORNGO	EVSCT	WVNAT	ACEDU	ACGRO	0	0	0	Y2002
#083	JOHANS	FAM06	AUSCI AUACA	ORNGO ORUNI	EVDAT	WVNAT	ACEMI	0	0	0	0	Y1999
#088	MINNES	FAM06	0	ORNGO	EVCAS EVDAT	WVMOD	ACEMI	ACNRG	0	0	0	Y2002
#091	CLEANW	FAM06	0	ORNGO	EVDAT EVPAN	WVECO	ACEMI	ACRST	0	0	0	Y2003
#093	SOCIET	FAM06	0	ORCHU	EVTHE	WVREL	ACEMI	ACTEC	0	0	0	Y1998
#098	HANSEN	FAM06	AUSCI	ORRES	EVSCT EVDAT	WVMOD	ACEMI	ACTEC	0	0	0	Y2000
#014	ROSENZ	FAM07	AUSCI	ORGOV	EVDAT	WVMOD WVNAT	ACADA	ACALA	0	0	0	Y1995
#032	STAKHI	FAM07	AUSCI	ORGOV	EVSCT	WVMOD	ACTEC	ACINT	0	0	0	Y1998
#048	IPCTHR	FAM07	AUSCI	ORNGO	EVSCT EVDAT	WVMOD	ACADA	ACMON	ACRCH	ACMDL	0	Y2001
#067	UKCLIM	FAM07	AUSCI	ORGOV	EVPAN	WVMOD	ACNRG	ACALA	0	0	0	Y2003
#015	EDMOND	FAM08	AUSCI	ORNGO	EVUTI EVDAT	WVECN	ACETR	0	0	1	0	Y1999
#027	TOMANM	FAM08	AUSCI	0	EVUTI	WVECN	ACEMI	ACADA	ACNEG	0	0	Y2001
#028	INOVES	FAM08	AUTRA	ORIND	EVDAT EVPAN	WVMOD	ACETR	ACRCH	ACINC	1	0	Y2002
#051	LINDEN	FAM08	0	0	EVANE	WVNAT	ACEGA	0	0	0	0	Y2003
#062	SHACKE	FAM08	AUSCI	ORGOV	EVSCT	WVMOD	ACEQU	ACNRG	0	0	0	Y2003
#017	RESPON	FAM09	AUSCI AUACA	ORGOV ORUNI	EVCAS EVANE	WVMOD	ACADA	ACSUS	ACNRG	0	1	Y2002
#029	PREPAR	FAM09	AUSCI	ORGOV	EVDAT	WVMOD	ACINT	ACEDU	ACINC	ACMDL	0	Y2000

DocNum	DocName	FAM	AU	OR	EV	WV	AC1	AC2	AC3	AC4	AC5	Y
#043	KOTEEN	FAM09	AUENV	ORRES ORNGO	EVSCT EVPIX	WVECO WVMOD	ACEMI	ACADA	0	0	0	Y2001
#045	WWFCCP	FAM09	0	ORNGO	EVSCT EVDAT	WVNAT	ACEMI	ACKYO	ACADA	ACEDU	ACEGA	Y2003
#057	HAYESD	FAM09	AUENV	ORNGO	EVDAT	WVNAT	ACEMI	ACTEC	ACINC	0	0	Y2000
#076	DESSAI	FAM09	AUENV	ORNGO	EVHIS EVSCT EVDAT	WVSCO	ACEMI	ACADA	ACEQU	0	0	Y2002
#077	BRAASC	FAM09	0	ORNGO ORUNI	EVSCT EVDAT EVPIX	WVNAT	ACEMI	ACBAC	ACSUS	0	1	Y2003
#084	SHOVEE	FAM09	AUSCI	ORUNI	EVDAT EVTHE	WVSCO	ACSCE	0	0	0	0	Y1996
#090	CAMPAI	FAM09	0	ORNGO	EVSCT EVEXP	WVMOD	ACEMI	0	0	0	0	Y1997
#099	WISCON	FAM09	0	ORGOV	EVSCT EVANE	WVNAT	ACEMI	ACSNK	0	0	0	0
#001	AGARWA	FAM10	AUENV	ORNGO	EVHIS EVRIT	WVECN WVMOR	ACPAY	ACPCE	0	0	0	Y1996
#004	RAYNER	FAM10	AUSCI	ORRES	EVANE EVMET	WVSCO	ACINT	ACAFF	0	0	0	Y1998
#006	JAMIES	FAM10	AUACA	ORUNI	EVHIS EVPAN	WVMOR	ACEQU	ACPCE	0	0	0	Y2001
#011	AHMEDQ	FAM10	AUENV	ORNGO	EVDAT	WVECO WVNAT	ACINT	ACEQU	0	0	0	Y2000
#016	GREENW	FAM10	AUENV	ORNGO	EVCAS	WVMOD	ACAFF	0	0	0	0	Y2001
#018	GLANTZ	FAM10	AUSCI	ORRES ORGOV	EVSCT EVMET	WVSCO	ACEDU	ACRCH	0	0	0	Y2001
#021	RIBOTJ	FAM10	AUSCI	ORNGO ORUNI	EVRIT EVCAS	WVMOR	ACEQU	ACHST	0	0	0	Y1996
#031	BOEHME	FAM10	AUSCI	0	EVPAN	WVPLY	ACNEG	0	0	0	0	Y1994
#033	QUICKM	FAM10	0	ORCHU	EVRIT	WVMOR	ACBAC	ACEQU	ACPCE	ACCNC	0	Y2003
#036	SOKONA	FAM10	AUSCI	ORNGO	EVSCT	WVMOR WVPLY	ACEMI	ACEQU	ACPCE	ACNEG	0	Y2002
#037	GYAWAL	FAM10	AUSCI	ORGOV	EVDAT EVPAN	WVNAT	ACTEC	ACMON	ACRCH	0	0	Y1996
#044	LAVINA	FAM10	AUENV	ORNGO	EVDAT EVPAN	WVPLY WVNAT	ACADA	ACEQU	ACAFF	ACEDU	0	Y2002
#061	CHANDL	FAM10	AUSCI	ORNGO	EVDAT EVEXP	WVECN	ACEMI	ACMON	ACFND	0	0	Y1997
#063	CHATTE	FAM10	AUACA	ORIND ORUNI	EVHIS EVSCT EVEXP EVPAN	WVNAT	ACINT	ACSUS	ACRST	0	1	Y1994
#066	MCMICH	FAM10	AUSCI	ORNGO	EVSCT EVDAT	WVNAT	ACEMI	ACPOP	ACEQU	0	0	Y1993
#078	HUQSAL	FAM10	AUSCI	ORNGO	EVPAN	WVMOD	ACADA	ACNEG	0	0	0	Y2001
#080	UNFAIR	FAM10	AUPOL	ORGOV	EVRIT	WVMOD	ACDIF	ACINT		0	0	Y1997
#094	MULLER	FAM10	AUTRA	0	EVDAT EVPAN	WVMOR WVPLY	ACAFF	0	0	0	0	Y2002
#008	MEADOW	FAM11	AUACA	ORUNI	EVMET	WVECO	ACRST	0	0	0	0	Y1997
#012	GOREAL	FAM11	AUPOL	ORGOV	EVHIS EVANE	WVECO WVNAT	ACINT	ACRST	0	0	0	Y1992
#025	BERGER	FAM11	AUSCI	0	EVSCT EVMET	WVNAT	ACEMI	ACINC	0	0	0	Y2000
#035	NRDCOU	FAM11	0	ORNGO	EVSCT EVDAT	WVNAT	ACEMI	ACNEG	0	0	0	Y2002
#042	SCHARP	FAM11	AUACA	ORUNI	EVHIS EVMET	WVNAT WVREL	ACBAC	ACRST	0	0	0	Y2002

DocNum	DocName	FAM	AU	OR	EV	WV	AC1	AC2	AC3	AC4	AC5	Y
#050	MEYERA	FAM11	AUACA	0	EVSCT EVPAN	WVNAT	ACRST	ACEDU	ACNRG	0	0	Y1993
#052	NWFEDE	FAM11	0	ORNGO	EVSCT	WVECO	ACEMI	ACINC	0	0	0	Y2000
#055	SUZUKI	FAM11	AUSCI	ORNGO	EVSCT	WVNAT	ACEMI	ACKYO	0	0	0	Y2002
#056	FOEINT	FAM11	0	ORNGO	EVSCT EVANE	WVNAT	ACKYO	ACEQU	ACPCE	0	0	Y2000
#058	ADHIKA	FAM11	0	ORNGO	EVDAT EVEXP	WVMOD	ACFND	0	0	0	0	Y2002
#064	PLUMWO	FAM11	AUACA	ORUNI	EVANE	WVSCO	ACEQU	ACRST	0	0	0	Y1993
#070	HARRER	FAM11	AUACA	ORUNI	EVHIS EVCAS	WVMOR WVSCO	ACEQU	ACNEG	0	0	0	Y1999
#071	CONWAY	FAM11	AUACA	ORUNI	EVTHE	WVSCO	ACNRG	ACHST	0	0	0	Y1999
#072	WORSTE	FAM11	AUACA	ORUNI	EVHIS EVMET	WVSCO	ACBAC	ACRST	ACINC	0	0	Y1999
#092	MCKIBB	FAM11	AUSCI	ORUNI	EVTHE	WVECO WVREL	ACSUS	ACSCE	0	0	1	Y2001

Appendix 2
Documents Listed by Argument

Climate Change Is Not a Problem

#23: Calder, N. (1999) 'The carbon dioxide thermometer and the cause of global warming', *Energy and Environment*, vol 10, no 1, pp1–18

#30: Singer, S. F. (2000) Interview, www.pbs.org/wgbh/warming/debate/singer.html

#46: Lindzen, R. S. (no date) *Global Warming: The Origin and Nature of the Alleged Scientific Consensus*, Cato Institute, Washington, DC

Climate Change Could Be Good for You

#3: Ausubel, J. H. (2001) 'Some ways to lessen worries about climate', *The Electricity Journal*, January/February, pp24–33

#23: Idso, C. D. and Idso, K. E. (2002) 'Carbon dioxide and global warming: Where we stand on the issue', www.co2science.org/about/position/globalwarming.htm

#34: 'API's position', downloaded March 2003 (but still refers to the Clinton Administration), www.api.org/globalclimate/apipos.htm

#59: Council for Agricultural Science and Technology (CAST) (1992) 'Preparing US agriculture for global climate change', Report 119, CAST, Ames, IO

#73: US Department of State (2003) 'United States global climate change policy', Fact Sheet, 27 February, www.state.gov/g/oes/rls/fs/2003/18055.htm

#74: Coon, C. E. (2002) 'President Bush's climate change proposal', WebMemo #83, The Heritage Foundation, 6 March, www.heritage.org/Research/EnergyandEnvironment/WM83.cfm?renderforprint=1

#81: 'Global warming – A corporate perspective' 'Newshour' transcript, 5 December 1997, www.pbs.org/newshour/bb/environment/july-dec97/air_12-5.html

#87: 'What about the effects of coal burning on climate?', The Greening Earth Society, www.bydesign.com/fossilfuels/crisis/html/climate_change.html

Science Can Solve This Problem

#9: Martens, W. J. M., Rotmans, J. and Niessen, L. W. (1994) *Climate Change and Malaria Risk: An Integrated Modelling Approach*, GLOBO Report Series No 3, Rijksinstituut voor Volksgezondheid en Milieuhygiene, Bilthoven, The Netherlands

#19: Darwin, R., Tsigas, M., Lewandrowski, J. and Raneses, A. (1996) 'Land use and cover in ecological economics', *Ecological Economics*, vol 17, pp157–181

#38: Cohen, S. J. (1993) 'Climate change and climate impacts: Please don't confuse the two!', *Global Environmental Change*, vol 3, no 1, pp2–6

#39: Ecimovic, T., Stuhler, E. A., Vezjak, M. and Mulej, M. (2002) 'Introduction to climate change – Present experience related to sustainability and impact on society', InfoAndina, www.mtnforum.org/emaildiscuss/discuss02/040102377.htm

#41: Van Asselt, M. B. A. and Rotmans, J. (2002) 'Uncertainty in integrated assessment modelling: From positivism to pluralism', *Climatic Change*, vol 54, pp75–105

#53: Parks, N. (2002) 'Measuring climate change', *BioScience*, vol 52, no 8, p652

#54: Taubes, G. (1997) 'Apocalypse not', *Science*, vol 278, pp1004–1006

#85: Slade, Ambassador, T. N. (2000) 'Linking science and climate change policy', Overview Address at the Pacific Islands Climate Change Conference, Rarotonga, Cook Islands, 3–7 April

#86: Ashford, G. and Castleden, J. (2001) 'Inuit observations on climate change: Final report', Institute for Sustainable Development, www.iisd.org/casl/projects/inuitobs.htm

More Modernization Is the Answer – Policy

#2: Benedick, R. E. (2001) 'Striking a new deal on climate change', *Issues in Science and Technology*, Fall 2001, pp71–76

#5: Goulder, L. H. and Nadreau, B. M. (2002) 'International approaches to reducing greenhouse gas emissions', in S. H. Schneider, A. Rosencranz and J. O. Niles (eds) *Climate Change Policy: a Survey*, Island Press, Washington, DC

#13: Edwards, P. (1996) 'Models in the policy arena', in S. J. Hassol and J. Katzenberger (eds) *Elements of Change, Session 2: Characterizing and Communicating Scientific Uncertainty*, Aspen Global Change Institute, Aspen, CO

#20: Athanasiou, T. (2003) 'Two futures, and a choice', *Progressive Response*, March, www.fpif.org/commentary/2003/0303choice.html

#60: Sandalow, D. B. and Bowles, I. A. (2001) 'Fundamental of treaty-making on climate change', *Science*, vol 292, pp1839–1840

#75: Robinson, D. (2002) 'Environmentalists criticize Bush climate change policy', *VOA News*, 15 February, http://greennature.com/article839.html

#79: Blanchard, O., Criqui, P., Trommetter, M. and Viguier, L. (2001) *Equity and Efficiency in Climate Change Negotiations: A Scenario for World Emission Entitlements by 2030*, Cahier de recherché No 26, Institute d'économie et de politique de l'énergie, Grenoble, France, www.upmf-grenoble.fr/iepe

#97: Worldwatch Institute (2002) 'Global war on global warming heats up', press release, www.worldwatch.org/press/news/2002/08/01

More Modernization – Energy-Related Change

#10: *USEA/USAID* (1999) *Handbook of Climate Change Mitigation Options for Developing Country Utilities and Regulatory Agencies*, Energy Resources International, Inc., Washington, DC

#24: Hoffert, M. I., Caldeira, K., Benford, G., Criswell, D. R., Green, C., Herzog, H., Jain, A. K., Kheshgi, H. S., Lackner, K. S., Lewis, J. S., Lightfoot, H. D., Manheimer, W., Mankins, J. C., Mauel, M. E., Perkins, L. J., Schlesinger, M. E., Volk, T. and Wigley, T. M. L. (2002) 'Advanced technology paths to global climate stability: Energy for a greenhouse planet', *Science*, vol 298, pp981–987

#26: Kawashima, Y. (2000) 'Nuclear power and climate change: The current situation in Japan and a message to the United States', Resources for the Future, www.weathervane.rff.org/pop/pop9/kwashima.html

#65: Porritt, J. (2003) 'Take action or climate change programme will fail to deliver', press notice, 12 February, www.sd-commission.gov/uk/events/news/pressrel/030212.htm

#68: The World Energy Modernization Plan, www.heatisonline.org/contentserve

#82: Global Environmental Facility and the United Nations Development Programme (1997) 'Capacity building for the rapid commercialization of renewable energy', project description

#89: Kirby, A. (1999) 'Nuking climate change', BBC News, 4 June, http://news.bbc.co.uk/1/hi/sci/tech/368584.stm

#95: German Advisory Council on Global Change (WBGU) (2003) 'World in transition – Towards sustainable energy systems', executive summary, www.wbgu.de/wbgu_jg2003_kurz_engl.html

#96: Department of Energy, Office of Fossil Energy (no date, but after May 1999) 'Carbon sequestration', www.fe.doe.gov/coal_power/sequestration/index.shtml

#100: Meadows, D. (1999) 'Amory Lovins sees the future and it is hydrogen', *The Global Citizen*, 4May, http://iisd.ca/pcdf/meadows/hydrogen.html

More Modernization – Economic Solution

#15: Edmonds, J., Scott, M. J. et al (1999) *International Emissions Trading and Global Climate Change*, Pew Center on Global Climate Change, Washington, DC

#27: Toman, M. A. (no date) 'Climate change economics and policies: An overview', retrieved from Resources for the Future website (www.rff.org) 12 March 2003 (last date in reference list is 2000)

#28: Inovest Strategic Value Advisors (2002) 'COE Briefing from *Climate Change and the Financial Services Industry*', United Nations Environment Programme Finance Initiatives, www.unepfi.net

#51: Linden, E. (2003) 'Who's going to pay for climate change?', *Time* 7 February

#62: Shackleton, R. G. (2003) *The Economics of Climate Change: A Primer*, Congress of the United States, Congressional Budget Office, Washington, DC, www.cbo.gov

More Modernization – Mitigation

#7: Meyerson, F. A. B. (2002) 'Population and climate change policy', in S. H. Schneider, A. Rosencranz and J. O. Niles (eds) *Climate Change Policy: A Survey*, Island Press, Washington, DC

#40: Sathaye, J. A. and Ravindranath, N. H. (1998) 'Climate change mitigation in the energy and forestry sectors of developing countries', *Annual Review of Energy and the Environment*, vol 23, pp287–437

#47: Browne, J. (1997) 'Climate change speech', Stanford University, http://icc370.igc.org/bp.htm

#49: 'Summary for policymakers 2001', in *Climate Change 2001: Mitigation*, a report of Working Group III of the Intergovernmental Panel on Climate Change, Cambridge University Press, Cambridge, UK

#69: Burnett, H. S. (2002) 'Ask the expert', Global Warming Hotline, National Center for Policy Analysis, http://globalwarming.ncpa.org/askthex/

#83: Johansen, B. E. (1999) Review of *Global Warming: The Essential Facts*, http://nativeamericas.aip.cornell.edu/fall99/fall99r.html

#88: Minnesotans for an Energy-Efficient Economy (ME3) (2002) 'Policies for a clean future: Greening our electricity industry', www.me3.org/issues/climate/withfire2002.html

#91: 'Clean water action', (no date, but internal evidence that it was written post-29 January 2003), Renewable Energy/Climate Change, www.cleanwateraction.org/ct/energy.html

#93: Society, Religion and Technology Project (1998) 'International petition to governments of industrialized countries', Church of Scotland, www.srtp.org.uk/climpet2.htm

#98: Hansen, J., Sato, M., Ruedy, R., Lacis, A. and Oinas, V. (2000) 'Global warming in the twenty-first century: An alternative scenario', *Proceedings of the National Academy of Sciences*, vol 97, pp9875–9880, www.giss.nasa.gov/gpol/abstracts/2000/HansenSatoR.html

More Modernization – Adaptation

#14: Rosenzweig, C. and Hillel, D. (1995) 'Potential impacts of climate change on agriculture and food supply', *Consequences: The Nature & Implications of Environmental Change*, vol 1, no 2, pp22–32

#32: Stakhiv, E. and Schilling, K. (1998) 'What can water managers do about global warming?', *Water Resources Update*, vol 112, pp3–40

#48: 'Summary for Policymakers 2001', in *Climate Change 2001: Impacts, Adaptation, and Vulnerability*, a report of Working Group II of the Intergovernmental Panel on Climate Change, Cambridge University Press, Cambridge, UK

#67: UK Climate Impacts Programme, Department for Environment Food and Rural Affairs, and Environment Agency (2003) *Climate Adaptation: Risk, Uncertainty and Decision-Making*, UKCIP, Oxford, UK, www.ukcip.org.uk

More Modernization – Both Mitigation and Adaptation

#17: 'Response strategies: Building resilience in systems' (2002) Chapter V in *The Potential Consequences of Climate Variability and Change for California: The California Regional Assessment*, University of California, Santa Barbara, CA

#29: *Preparing for a Changing Climate: The Potential Consequences of Climate Variability and Change, Mid-Atlantic Overview* (2000) Mid-Atlantic Regional Assessment Team, Pennsylvania State University, University Park, PA

#43: Koteen, L., Bloomfield, J., Eichler, T., Tonne, C., Young, R., Poulshock, H. and Sosler, A. (2001) *Hot Prospects: The Potential Impacts of Global Warming on Los Angeles and the Southland*, Executive Summary, Introduction, first two chapters, Environmental Defense, Washington, DC, www.environmentaldefense.org

#45: World Wide Fund 'Climate change programme 2003', www.panda.org/about_wwf/what_we_do/climate_change/problems/index.cfm

#57: Hayes, D. (2000) *The Official Earth Day Guide to Planet Repair*, Island Press, Washington, DC

#76: Dessai, S. (2002) *The Special Climate Change Fund: Origins and Prioritization*, the Tyndall Centre for Climate Change Research and EURONATURA Centre for Environmental Law and Sustainable Development, Lisbon

#77: Braasch, G. (2003) 'World view of global warming', www.worldviewofglobalwarming.org/

#84: Shove, E. (1996) *Working Back from the Future*, unpublished paper, Centre for the Study of Environmental Change, Lancaster University, UK

#90: Campaign for Nuclear Phaseout (1997) 'Nuclear power is not the solution to climate change', 28 November, www.ccnr.org/no_nukes_cnp.html

#99: Department of Natural Resources, Wisconsin (no date) 'Global warming is hot stuff!', www.dnr.state.wi.us/org/caer/ce/eek/earth/air/global.htm, retrieved 8 June 2003

The Problem Is Inequality

#1: Agarwal, A. and Narain, S. (1996) *The Atmospheric Rights of All People on Earth: Why Is It Necessary to Move Towards the 'Ultimate Objective' of the Framework Convention on Climate Change?*, Centre for Science and the Environment, www.cseindia.org/html/cmp/cmp31.htm

#4: Rayner, S. and Malone, E. L. (1998) 'Ten suggestions for policymakers', in S. Rayner and E. L. Malone (eds) *Human Choice and Climate Change, Vol. 4: What Have We Learned?*, Battelle Press, Columbus, OH

#6: Jamieson, D. (2001) 'Climate change and global environmental justice', in C. A. Miller and P. N. Edwards (eds) *Changing the Atmosphere: Expert Knowledge and Environmental Governance*, MIT Press, Cambridge, MA

#11: Ahmed, Q. K. and Ahmed, A. U. (2000) 'Social sustainability, indicators and climate change', in *Climate Change and Its Linkages with Development, Equity and Sustainability: Proceedings of the IPCC Expert Meeting held in Columbo, Sri Lanka, 27–29 April 1999*, World Bank, Washington, DC

#16: Greenwald, J., Roberts, B. and Reomer, A. D. (2001) *Community Adjustment to Climate Change Policy*, Pew Center on Global Climate Change, Washington, DC

#18: Glantz, M. H. (2001) 'Editorial: Global warming yea-sayers and naysayers: Time to bridge the gap?', *Network Newsletter*, Climate-Related Impacts International Network (NCAR and NOAA)

#21: Ribot, J. C. (1996) 'Introduction: Climate variability, climate change and vulnerability: Moving forward by looking back', in J. C. Ribot, A. R. Magalhães and S. S. Panagides, *Climate Variability, Climate Change and Social Vulnerability in the Semi-arid Tropics*, Cambridge University Press, Cambridge, UK

#31: Boehmer-Christiansen, S. (1994) 'Global climate protection policy: The limits of scientific advice', Parts 1 and 2, *Global Environmental Change*, vol 4, no 2, pp140–159 and vol 4, no 3, pp185–200

#33: Quick, M. (no date) 'Friends and climate change – Contraction and convergence?', www.quakergreenconcern.org.uk/displayarticle.asp?artcleid, downloaded March 2003

#36: Sokona, Y., Najam, A. and Huq, S. (2002) 'Climate change and sustainable development: Views from the South', and Huq, S., Sokona, Y. and Najam, A. (2002) 'Climate change and sustainable development beyond Kyoto', International Institute for Environment and Development (IIED), www.iied.org

#37: Gyawali, D. (1996) 'An extreme climate event in Nepal and its implications for a climate change regime', in *Elements of Change 1995*, Aspen Global Change Institute, Aspen, CO

#44: La Vina, A. G. M. (2002) 'From Kyoto to Marrakech: Global climate politics and local communities', working paper, World Resources Institute, Washington, DC, and New York

#61: Chandler, W. (1997) *The Economic Rewards of 'No Regrets' Climate Policies*, Conference on Strengthening the Russian Economy through Climate Change Policies, United Nations Environment Program, Moscow

#63: Chatterjee, P. and Finger, M. (1994) 'The Framework Convention on Climate Change' and 'Conclusions', in *The Earth Brokers: Power, Politics and World Development*, Routledge, London

#66: McMichael, A. J. (1993) *Planetary Overload: Global Environmental change and the Health of the Human Species*, Cambridge University Press, Cambridge, UK (especially 'Introduction', 'Greenhouse warming and climate change' and 'The way ahead')

#78: Huq, S. (2001) 'Climate change conference in Bonn: What does it mean for Bangladesh?', retrieved 29 May 2003 from the internet

#80: 'Unfair burden?' (1997) 'Newshour' transcript, 9 December, www.pbs.org/newshour/bb/environment/july-dec97/india_12-9.html

#94: Müller, B. (2002) *Equity in Climate Change: The Great Divide*, Oxford Institute for Energy Studies, www.ejcc.org/resources_tech.html

The Problem Is Modern People/Nature Relationship

#8: Meadows, D. H. (1997) 'Mother Gaia reflects on the global climate conference', http://csf.colorado.edu/forums/ecofem/dec97/0009.html

#12: Gore, A. (1992) *Earth in the Balance: Ecology and the Human Spirit*, Houghton Mifflin, New York

#25: Berger, J. J. (2000) *Beating the Heat: Why and How We Must Combat Global Warming*, Berkeley Hills Books, Berkeley, CA

#35: Natural Resources Defense Council (2002) 'Untangling the accounting gimmicks in White House global warming and pollution plans', wysiwyg://14/http://www.nrdc.org/globalwarming/agwcon.asp

#42: Scharper, S. B. (2002) 'Green dreams: Religious cosmologies and environmental commitments', *Bulletin of Science, Technology and Society*, vol 22, no 1, pp42–44

#50: Meyer-Abich, K. M. (1993) 'Winners and losers in climate change', in W. Sachs (ed) *Global Ecology: A New Arena of Political Conflict*, Zed Books, London

#52: National Wildlife Federation (2000) 'Climate change', in *The Toll from Coal: How Emissions from the Nation's Coal-Fired Power Plants Devastate Wildlife and Threaten Human Health*, National Wildlife Foundation, www.nwf.org

#55: Suzuki, D. (2002) 'Waiting to fight climate change is not a viable option', http://production.enn.com/extras/printer-friendly.asp?storyid+47610

#56: Friends of the Earth International (2000) *Gathering Storm: The Human Cost of Climate Change*, FoEI, London

#58: Adhikary, P. (2002) 'Climate change on the roof of the world', in *Tough Terrain: Media Reports of Mountain Issues*, Asia Pacific Mountain Network and Panos Institute South Asia, www.aias.org.au/pdfs_docs/newsletters/aias13.pdf

#64: Plumwood, V. (1993) *Feminism and the Mastery of Nature*, Routlege, London

#70: Harré, R., Brockmeier, J. and Mühlhäusler, P. (1999) *Greenspeak: a Study of Environmental Discourse*, Sage, Thousand Oaks, CA (especially pp22–23, 61–68, 115–116 and 173–188)

#71: Conway, J. K., Keniston, K. and Marx, L. (1999) 'The new environmentalisms', in J. K. Conway, K. Keniston and L. Marx (eds) *Earth, Air, Fire, Water: Humanistic Studies of the Environment*, University of Massachusetts Press, Amherst, MA

#72: Worster, D. (1999) 'Climate and history: Lessons from the Great Plains', in J. K. Conway, K. Keniston and L. Marx (eds) *Earth, Air, Fire, Water: Humanistic Studies of the Environment*, University of Massachusetts Press, Amherst, MA

#92: McKibben, B. (2001) 'Where do we go from here?', *Daedalus* special issue, 'Religion and ecology: Can the climate change?', www.daedelus.amacad.org/issues/fall2001/mckibben.htm

Index